NO AVATARS
ALLOWED

NO AVATARS ALLOWED

THEOLOGICAL REFLECTIONS ON VIDEO GAMES

JOSHUA WISE

CHURCH
PUBLISHING
INCORPORATED

References:
Pages 11–12: Alfred, Lord Tennyson, "In Memoriam A.H.H."
(London: Edward Moxon, Dover Street, 1850).
Page 57: Walt Whitman, "O Me! O Life!," *Leaves of Grass*
(Philadelphia: David McKay Publisher, 1891–92), 215.
Page 58: G. K. Chesterton, *Orthodoxy* (New York: John Lane Company, 1914), 85.
Page 124: Alfred, Lord Tennyson, "Ulysses," *Poems,* vol. 2
(London: Edward Moxon, Dover Street, 1842).
Page 151: *Pastoral Constitution on the Church in the Modern World*
(Washington, DC: United States Catholic Conference, 1965).

Church Publishing
19 East 34th Street
New York, NY 10016
www.churchpublishing.org

Cover design by Paul Soupiset
Typesetting and page design by Beth Oberholtzer

A record of this book is available from the Library of Congress.

ISBN-13: 978-1-64065-184-5 (pbk.)
ISBN-13: 978-1-64065-185-2 (ebook)

*To my brother, Matthew, who has been
my companion on many adventures.*

*To Fr. Ben, who has been my fellow explorer
in these wild new worlds of inquiry.*

To Fr. Dave, with whom I have journeyed far.

*And to Sarah, who has been my
constant support in this effort.*

CONTENTS

FOREWORD

How many things in life can you say are truly consistent?

Life is incredible in its ability to be both shockingly turbulent and remarkably steady. It's in the tension between those opposites that we are molded and shaped into who we will become. The origin story of *No Avatars Allowed* takes place between those two opposites.

I met Dr. Joshua Wise on orientation day at the Lutheran Theological Seminary in Philadelphia almost a decade ago. I was still a bright-eyed seminarian heading toward ordination, and he was a masters student ready to challenge expectations and professors on his way to fulfilling his calling of teaching theology. We were strangers in a strange new place, who bonded over coincidences: we both studied at Eastern University as undergraduate students; we had known some of the same professors; we were both from the Episcopal tradition though studying in a Lutheran setting; and, perhaps most importantly, we both held a lifelong love of video games.

Video games would be the shared joy to bind our friendship together. That day, I could never have guessed the chance meeting would change my life so drastically and influence so many future days and decisions. I had no idea we would start podcasting together, sharing our love of God and games with the world on the *No Avatars Allowed* podcast. I could never have dreamed that, even further down the road, podcasting would become my passion and pride, shaping so much of my life and career. And the idea that Josh and I would eventually live together in intentional community and serve in parish ministry together, PhD and priest, would have then likely seemed absurd.

That was the journey ahead of us, and the road between then and now has been filled with epic challenges—achievements unlocked, goals accomplished, others failed, heartbreak, laughter, and loss shared, and so much more.

Some of my best memories are of those early days of *No Avatars Allowed*. We built a podcast and a friendship on hours of *StarCraft* online play, *Call of Duty* special ops, midnight releases at Game Stop, laughing at horrible press releases, and teaching church councils and sacraments. I learned more theology and church history from Josh doing those podcasts than I did in the seminary classroom. Even then, before his PhD program, Josh was one of the most knowledgeable and well-read theologians I had ever met. He taught me to keep thinking about what I was playing; during those days I thought more deeply about my faith than I ever had before—and perhaps since.

I remember those days as much simpler times. When Josh and I first met, I was happily married and studying at Lutheran seminary just long enough to transfer to an Episcopal school to finish my seminary training and become ordained. That path took me through the birth of my oldest daughter, two ordinations, and a devastating first call that shook my faith and my marriage to the core.

Josh and I built *No Avatars Allowed* along the way until my own journey deviated too far and I left the podcast. The show changed format and eventually ended. Our friendship became strained by disappointment and distance. The years after that contained so many changes. Josh defended his dissertation and graduated from Catholic University in a remarkably short amount of time. Both of us lived through the pain of divorce, and the self-discovery and meaning-making that comes afterward.

We launched a new ministry together, an intentional community designed to serve the small parish where I am rector. And, there, living and serving together it became clear: it was time to resurrect *No Avatars Allowed*. Through all of the changes in each of our lives, from that first chance meeting to the reboot of the podcast, these things remained the same: our love of games and how much fun we have talking about them.

This is not just an origin story, but the heart of this book. Games aren't just some silly pasttime. From childhood to adulthood, play is the psychological space where we process transition and our ability to cope with the challenges of the world around us. That tension between turbulence and consistency is what psychoanalyst D.W. Winnicott described as the psychic space of transition. It is a child leaving their mother to go play and explore, while always safely returning home for reassurance. This is the same psychic space where we play out our relationship with God.

I know of no one who has thought more about the philosophical and theological implications of the intersection of video games and theology, particularly from an orthodox Christian perspective, than Dr. Joshua Wise. He has taught, thought, and written about how games can reveal philosophical concepts to us with implications for our reality, about how this kind of play has the power to change us and reveal to us ourselves and therefore our God.

Thinking of the distinctions between my own level of reality as a player and the reality of the world generated in a video game, and the interaction between myself and my avatar between these levels of reality, has helped me better understand the vastly difficult concept of God's relationship to Creation. Not just a philosophical concept, this way of thinking about levels of existence directly affects my own understanding of my relationship, my dependence on the Eternal God who is not a limited, finite creature like me. While outside Creation,

God also interacts with my world in a way that brings about the plan of salvation.

Beyond thinking philosophically this way, Joshua Wise has helped me personally understand more fully the power and importance of the good news of Jesus. He has been consistently my friend and brother along the way through some of the most difficult challenges life has presented. And, as a priest, I've learned through all of this the importance of embracing the things that bring you joy in life as a way to engage in ministry that is passionate and authentic. If the world is playing video games, the church needs to meet people there.

I'm thrilled that the work Joshua Wise has done with video games and theology will now make its way from podcast to print, as well as for the opportunity to introduce him and this work to you. I know that, if you take this book seriously, you will discover how the kind of fun and joyful play that video games offer us can also become thought-provoking and life-changing. It is good news that God has given us the joy of these games, as they reveal to us God's Son.

How many things in your life can you say are truly consistent?

I give thanksgiving to God for the love of games, for deep friendship that shares that joy and love, and for *No Avatars Allowed* going strong almost a decade after its start. May the ideas of this book, and the brilliant writing of Dr. Joshua Wise delivering them to you, bless your life the way they have blessed mine.

Father Benjamin Gildas, AF

INTRODUCTION

Friends, Learning, and Gaming

Many of my friends are priests and minsters. They are Catholic, Lutheran, Methodist, and Episcopalian. They are women and men, older and younger than I. And the thing that literally every one of them has in common is that they play games. Not all of them play video games, but all of them are "gamers." For some of them, games are their main hobby; some of them engage in the pastime whenever they can. But every one of them wakes up Sunday morning, administers word and sacrament, and, at some other point during their week or month, plays games. All of them have played modern board games. As far as I know, all of them have played pen and paper role-play games (and have yet to sell their souls to Satan or join a cult). The vast majority of them have fired guns at the simulacra of human beings in video games. All of them do this and then go minister to God's people, unhindered by their play.

The greatest friendships of my life have often involved the blending of two main interests: theology and gaming. Friends I made in college, at jobs, in seminary, and in my PhD program have all gathered around games of one kind or another. We played together, argued about religion together, and built lasting friendships together. Indeed, the one constant, other than education and friendship, in all the institutions of higher learning I attended was gaming. In college, we sat around and played *Mario Kart 64* and *GoldenEye* on a Nintendo 64. In seminary, we traded stories of *Minecraft* and played characters in role-play games. In my PhD program, we had a group who played it all—horror board games, old and new video games, and *Dungeons & Dragons*. With the exception of a few college buddies, I still play with these friends. Some of them live close by, and we game together a few times a month. Some are far away, and we use the miracle of the internet to catch up over video-chat and solve mysteries together for a couple of hours once every few weeks. We are all, unquestionably, geeks. We might not all look like the stereotype, but we love the experience of playing together so much that we often open our homes to total strangers to play with them. We make websites, write reviews, spend hours creating fantasy settings and adventures for each other, and we record podcasts. We love creating and engaging in the creations of our friends.

For many of us, we see these activities as parts of a grand Christian tradition: a romantic endeavor in which the great Arthurian stories were fashioned and the fantastical worlds of George MacDonald, J. R. R. Tolkien, and C. S. Lewis were crafted. We see ourselves as taking part in a spirituality of friendship that involves play. That doesn't mean we never play alone; we often do. But it is rare that we have great solitary experiences without coming back to our friends to say, "You have to hear what happened!"

Beyond friendship, gaming is a way in which we minister to our community. For about a year after I moved back to the Philadelphia area, I talked with my cohost of *No Avatars Allowed*, Fr. Ben Gildas, AF, who wrote the foreword to this book, about using his particular gifts and interests to form a ministry. He created a meetup for board games at our church, and the group immediately took off. Instead of fitting into a prior generation's mold of what a priest should be interested in or what he should look like, he took the particular gifts God has given him and made a welcoming space for people to play together.

This Book

This book is, in many ways, the result of these experiences of friendship, play, and reflection. I'm not just a Christian who games, but a theologian who games and wants to think seriously about what I play. And, as I keep thinking about what I have been playing, I keep coming back to the idea that video games are still in a place of estrangement and suspicion when it comes to the church.

This book is also the result of a series of accidents and idle conversations that have culminated in serious discussions about the value of video games for theological reflection. It is, in some ways, a book about what it means to be in that strange place called the church while being in the midst of culture. Of course, all church is experienced in the context of culture unless one escapes to a solitary cave and prays that no one else takes up in the cave next-door. Even then, we are immersed in the culture of our earlier years and must negotiate that relationship.

This book is about the negotiation between church and culture at the very specific point of video games. From their origins as novelties and experiments in engineering on cathode-ray-tubes and oscilloscopes to the multibillion-dollar earning products like *Grand Theft Auto V*, video games have had a strange and meteoric, though sometimes bumpy, rise to becoming one of the most prevalent forms of entertainment and expression. Often, the church met this new medium with suspicion and rejection. Video games have been viewed by the church as frivolous, dangerous, and generally unworthy of serious theological reflection. Indeed, when the church tends to view our world as merely a drab and dreary "veil of tears," the church has been suspicious of the very idea of play.

One need not look far to find denouncements of leisure time throughout Christian history. But such denouncements are a rejection of a comprehensive theological anthropology. In other words, they strip humanity of some of its most important component parts. Play is an important element of what it means to be human—not just what it means to be a child. The segregation of play (though not an entire segregation, for there are exceptions) into the life of children has a deeply privileged Victorian flavor to it. As Kimberley Reynolds, professor of children's literature at Newcastle Univeristy, has pointed out in her article "Perceptions of Childhood," while it is true that poorer Victorian children were sent to work in factories, the middle and upper classes of Victorian culture idolized childhood as innocent and angelic, elevating the domestic loves to nearly divine proportions. Correspondingly these classes "put aside childish things" at the advent of adulthood. Frivolities such as play were blessed, but must be set aside for the responsibilities of adult life. It took the wonders of people like Rev. Charles Dodgson and George MacDonald to buck the trend and offer a celebration of childlike wonder and childhood in the midst of the rigors of not only adulthood, but Christian adulthood.

Indeed, not only does play get relegated to the realm of childhood in worldviews like that of the Victorian period, but it loses any value as a subject of intellectual study or prayerful reflection. The very idea that play, and especially the specific kind of play that is the subject of this book—video games—might be taken seriously by adults has been an occasion for everything from bemusement to scorn, especially by the church.

This is, of course, changing. There are scholars of religion and gaming now. The study of play as a serious intellectual pursuit goes back at least to the foundational 1938 study of the play-element in culture, *Homo Ludens* by Johan Huizinga. There are now serious academic works on board games, role-playing games like *Dungeons & Dragons*, and video games. There are plenty of ministers who have grown up playing all these kinds of games and who continue to do so. Indeed, the church is now a place where many are playing some kind of game daily, whether on their phones, on a dedicated gaming console, or on their computers. Yet the stigma of video games remains. This book is an attempt to address that stigma in two distinct ways.

The first half of the book is an appeal to those within the church to be more open to the discussion of gaming. It will introduce several aspects of video games to those who either have not had the opportunity or the desire to engage with them. The second half is an expression of a few ways in which video games can contribute to our thinking as a church.

My goal is therefore twofold. My hope is that the first section will invite people within the church, especially those in positions of power, to look past whatever prejudices they might have about video games so that they can engage the second half of the book with an open mind. For those who do have that open mind, my hope is that the second half will be useful as a point of departure for reflection on the mysteries and doctrines of Christianity.

The mystery of God is infinite, and it seems useful to me that we should never disparage help when contemplating the mysteries of the sacraments and the Incarnation. As someone who has both grown up with video games and who has become a professor of systematic theology, it is my contention that video games can be of great use to us in this area.

This book will ask you to engage seriously with the question at hand. It will, I hope, offer in return insight into the goodness of video games, how the places where they aren't good can be helped by the church, and how they can help us think more clearly about some of the deepest questions in our theology. Beyond all of that, it offers a bridge between the old culture and the new one, as well as a blueprint for building future bridges that will help us cross over such a divide when the next thing comes along.

Theological Starting Points

I'm writing from within the tradition of the Episcopal Church, which has been my home for about fifteen years. My education ranges from progressive evangelical biblical studies to Lutheran systematic theology and, finally, Catholic systematic theology. I have spent the last fifteen or so years of my life as a computer programmer.

My theological convictions tend to lean toward the Christology and sotereology of the Greek Fathers. It is the coupling of the goodness and weakness of creation with the radical limitedness of human language to describe God that lies behind this book. Both Athanasius's view that the world is falling back into nothingness, and Gregory of Nyssa's arguments against Eunomius that no language can encompass God underpin these pages. There is a certain amount of Platonism, which I'll go into, and a certain amount of Cyril of Alexandria's Christology here as well. There's also some Thomas Aquinas sprinkled in, especially when it comes to questions of knowledge. Finally, there is a heaping of George MacDonald, who held that all creation is needful to set forth God in revelation. This includes the works of our hands, the creations of our imaginations, and the joyful moments we spend together. MacDonald knew well that two or three may gather in Christ's name to tell stories, play games, or even fly a kite to the glory of the Lord, and that God would certainly be in their midst.

GENERATIONS OF
BELIEVERS THAT GAME

Everyone Games

I don't remember when my father taught me to play chess.
He had been brought up in the Dogpatch and Tenderloin dis-
tricts of San Francisco and had seen several people murdered
in front of him before he was fifteen years old. I'm not sure
where he learned the game, but I know that he taught me to
play when I was young, how to move the knight differently
than the bishop, and how to castle. I remember that I was
young because by fifth grade I was learning, from my science
teacher, the gambit known as "fool's mate" and discovering for
myself how to move a pawn en passant.

This is not a story of a father with a rough upbringing teaching his son to play chess and, lo and behold, the father and
son were chess masters. Neither my father nor I were ever
very good at the game. He might have been, if he had put his
mind to it. Instead, we played now and then; I can't say that I
remember when our last chess game took place. It was probably on a family vacation when I was a teenager.

At some point in his very rough life—perhaps in prison—someone taught my father a game about military strategy abstracted into a small, eight-by-eight board in which bishops, no less, killed knights and common folk. The pawn, standing in for the hard-working farmer whose life was often of little worth to the landed nobles who waged their wars across the face of Europe, died easily. However, with good strategy, that pawn could become noble and mighty by reaching the other side of the board. Chess is a violent game, but the violence is abstracted far enough from the bloodshed of the medieval battlefield that we often put away any concerns about teaching children to play. The benefits of the game—strategic thinking, patience, forethought, sportsmanship—outweigh its bloody heritage.

Most every generation has played games that draw their inspirations from combat and war. Such games require thinking people to apply their minds openly and critically to what each form of play is saying about its culture, and what it teaches children. That children play at defeating evil is a good thing. C. S. Lewis points out that the training of our imaginations, the training of our reflexes, and the training of our virtues in play allow us to be readier for those situations in real life. But this training can go awry. When generations of white boys and girls played "Cowboys and Indians," the Native American peoples were placed in the role of the villain and the imaginations of children were conditioned to think incorrectly and disparagingly of other human beings.

Less problematic perhaps, though not without its difficulties, is the play of "cops and robbers." One can imagine, however, in the current American social climate, that the decision about who is good and who is bad might be up in the air for many children. When Electronic Arts, a prominent video game publisher, released the game *Battlefield Hardline* in 2015, a game of virtual "cops and robbers," many in the video game community criticized the game's seemingly tone-deaf attitude toward the hardline tactics of police against criminals while America was reeling from police violence.

One might object that play need not be violent. What about a tea party? What about playing at being explorers? It is true that a tea party need not involve a daring shoot-out between Mr. Bear and Ms. Bunny while Ms. Porcupine's best china is shattered to pieces and the tables and chairs are turned over for good cover. Though, I must admit that imagining Ms. Rabbit jumping up from behind a doily-covered sideboard and knocking the stuffing out of Mr. Owl with a bazooka presents an amusing picture.

But even if we pass on this Quentin Tarantino version of a tea party, this kind of play is not without its need for critique. What does the tea party say about our views of class, society, and money? Are the poor skunks invited to the tea party, or only the most perfumed of the woodland creatures? Do the turtles who do the drudgework for the rabbits who live in the big house get to sit and eat biscuits, or must they go back to their hovels as they have nothing fine to wear?

As for exploration, there is little to critique about bravery in the face of nature's dangers, but, whether it is exploration of the North Pole, a dangerous jungle, or a journey to the moon, the nasty context of nationalistic imperialism does tend to rear its head.

That is not to say that one might not play cops and robbers in which the police are just and brave. One might play at a tea party in which the poor are, as Christ commands, invited in to share in the vittles. One might assemble an international team to explore the jungle to make contact and create a fair trade relationship with the indigenous people. All of that is possible in play. But, being creatures who are fallen, we will find other ways of slipping our fallenness into our recreation, whether it is virtual or not.

Why We Should Care about Video Games

In one sense, video games are nothing new. They are play that is fun, inspirational, challenging, and in desperate need of critique. In another sense, they are genuinely novel. Things that once only existed in our imagination, on the page, or on film are now presented to us so that we can interact with them and examine them from all angles. They have the wonder of the greatest movie scenes and effects, the interactivity of our imaginations, and the permanence of a book.

Video games also give us the kind of feedback that we can otherwise only get in the real world. I might have my action figure punch another action figure, but my mind must provide all of the sounds, the bruising, and the impact of the hit. If I'm not given to a particularly gory imagination, perhaps when my Batman figure hits the Joker, the Joker gets a fat lip and falls to the ground. If I'm more inclined toward blood and guts, perhaps the damage is more extensive, more along the lines of a mature comic book or movie. In a video game, when Batman hits a criminal in the *Arkham* series by Rocksteady Games, the bone-crunching effect of the world's greatest combatant is visually and audibly clear. And, after a well-executed fight, I can sit back and think, "I did that," as the criminals lie on the street cradling their badly injured limbs.

All of this means that video games require more complex thought when we are critiquing them. Like drawn or animated art, they show us things that our imaginations probably don't conjure on their own. Like physical play, they respond to our actions: we have agency. Like choose-your-own-adventure books, there is some sense that we are working with someone else, someone who created the content, to tell our own story in a new world. Like chess, we must think strategically, and hopefully will engage in good sportsmanship and fair play.

Video games are a beast of complexity that the church must actively engage because the church is playing video games. Few pastors, however—Catholic, Protestant, or Orthodox—are particularly conversant with them. There may be a host of reasons for this, but my suspicion is that the main problem is that, at least within Christianity, a stigma remains attached to playing these games. Throughout my academic career, I have encountered this stigma repeatedly, but a few examples should suffice. During my PhD program, I took a class on the theology of grace. It was a relatively large seminar because the professor was popular. Across from me sat an intelligent, gym-going, newly minted Catholic priest. Before class started, I made a joke about having "a healthy video gaming habit." I meant that my habit of playing video games was alive and well and that I fed it regularly. The young priest took me to mean that I thought that my habit was healthy for me. I pointed out that that was not what I meant, but what if I had? He seemed to take it as given that video games were an unhealthy pastime. He made no argument for their lack of value other than the generalization that everyone knows they are to be shunned.

A few years earlier, when I was doing my MA in systematic theology at the Lutheran Theological Seminary at Philadelphia, an institution now absorbed into the United Lutheran Seminary, I remember mentioning to one of my professors that my friend Ben (now Father Ben, who wrote the foreword to this book) and I were doing a podcast on theology and video games. She laughed—and she was not the only professor to do so.

A final example will suffice for my point. About a year ago, after Mass, the same Father Ben and I were discussing a game night. This time it was board games and good, old-fashioned paper and pencil role play. One of the parishioners laughed and said, "What do you plan to do when you grow up?"

5

Each of these instances reveals two kinds of suspicion. The first, divorced from Christianity, is that video games are for children. The second is that video games are either so dangerous or so vapid that they do not warrant serious theological engagement. The first issue exists largely across a generational divide. Those who didn't grow up playing video games, and who haven't experienced them growing and changing, have little experience with the vast, mature, insanely complex worlds creadted by hundreds of adults for other adults to engage in. The second issue is largely due to an unexamined consensus that doesn't stand up to serious scrutiny, especially when compared with other accepted hobbies for adults.

I will not spend the rest of this chapter attempting to argue that those who didn't grow up with video games should try, if they can, to see past the generational gap in the same way that they perhaps hoped their parents would have with the music of their youth that has continued to entertain them throughout their lives. I will not spend paragraphs on the difficulties of spectator sports as a hobby that one picks up in one's youth and then carries all one's years. Instead, I want to contend that clergy and theologically minded people should take video games seriously because they are something that the church is doing. Many millions of people play video games; many of these people are religious.

Not only is the church playing video games, it's making them. Christians are actively involved in the creation of game worlds. A few years ago, I was researching *Past the Sky's Rim: The Elder Scrolls and Theology,* a book that looked at how theologians and scholars of religious studies could engage *The Elder Scrolls* by Bethesda Games. I got to sit down with one of the writers of the popular game *Skyrim* over coffee in Bethesda, Maryland, and talk about stories, the games in the series, and faith. He is a Christian who has had a good career making major video games. He is by no means alone.

The church plays games; the church makes games. It may be that not every congregation in America has gamers in it, but I would bet that most do. Our religious leaders need to be conversant in the popular literature of the day; the ever-expanding adventures in the worlds of Hyrule, Tamriel, Azeroth, and a thousand others are, for at least three generations of churchgoers, one major corpus.

Worlds That Engage Us

If we should take video games seriously, what is their substance? We might assume that all video games are something like *Pac-Man*, or like the violent shooting games we've seen on the news. And, there are a lot of games like *Pac-Man* and *Grand Theft Auto* out there. There are also games where you simply move a little picture around a screen, collect things, eat things, light things up, and put things in the correct order. There are games that are focused entirely on shooting other people in a virtual world. There are games that are focused on the activity of gameplay, and there are those that work to draw the player into an engaging story with interesting characters.

There are myriad other genres that draw players in. On the more militaristic side, there are strategy games in which you move pieces around a large map to try to take over territory, much like the board game *Risk*—or chess, come to think of it. There are games that involve flying planes, driving tanks, sailing ships, steering submarines, and commanding tank battalions or fleets of ships. In more imaginative settings, you might do all these things, except on a science fiction space-battlefield, or in a fantasy world. Instead of commanding the Soviet KV1 tank against Panzers in a World War II simulation, you might command the starships of *Star Trek*, the X-wings of *Star Wars*, or armies of elves or orcs in Tolkien's Middle Earth.

In narrative games such as *Gone Home, The Stanley Parable*, and *What Remains of Edith Finch*, the player interacts with the world around them to discover a story embedded in the game's environment. Sometimes this is done by way of spoken narrative, sometimes by text found in the world, and sometimes the player is invited simply to "read" the scene. These stories are often touching, personal, and melancholy. Sometimes they are uplifting; sometimes scary.

A popular kind of video game is the open-world role play. In this genre, the player is placed in an expansive world that can take hundreds of hours to explore. They are often challenged with quests by other characters they meet, challenged by hostile forces, and engaged in the discovery of fascinating locations and stories. Players often gain experience doing these things that translates into increased skills so that they can barter with people more effectively, repair their gear, use better weapons, construct equipment, talk people down from dangerous situations, and survive more damage. The more the player plays, the more capable their character becomes, so they can tackle even greater challenges. Games like *Fallout, The Witcher 3*, or *Breath of the Wild* are good examples of how aesthetically engaging these virtual worlds can be. They are filled with intricate detail, memorable characters, and surprising events.

Video games span the spectrum from pure puzzles to rich narratives. They ask us to think differently than we do in our regular lives, and they offer us experiences and vistas that don't exist in our world. From personal experience I can say that the spooky town of Silent Hill is a place that I love to visit virtually, but I wouldn't want to go walking down its deserted misty streets by myself in real life. The same can be said for Stephen King's Derry, Maine, or H. P. Lovecraft's Dunwich, Massachusetts. I enjoy walking through the postapocalyptic wasteland of the *Fallout* series, and enjoy movies like *Mad*

Max, The Book of Eli, and stories like "A Boy and His Dog." It should go without saying, though, that I am entirely opposed to anything that would turn our planet into a nuclear wasteland. In other words, video games engage all manner of our human capacities, and they often do so in ways that offer us experiences that we couldn't have otherwise.

Story Telling

Video games invite us to be active storytellers. They often require us to make choices, to see what the consequences are of those choices, and they invite us to share our stories with others. Much like the fans of football or baseball will replay the game the next morning, adding their own (unquestionably expert) opinions about how the game should have been played, gamers will talk about their own experiences playing alone or together.

A close friend of mine, who happens to be a priest, and I were playing a game called *Sea of Thieves*. In the game you are a pirate sailing the high seas, searching for treasure, fighting both skeletons and other players, and, for all intents and purposes, swashing every buckle you come across. The game was roundly criticized for not having a lot of structure when it first came out in 2018. Players were given different kinds of quests and then they would go off on their ships, either a sloop or a galleon, to dig up treasure, fight skeletons, or collect livestock. When they finished their quests, they returned to the people who sent them out and handed over the booty for rewards they could use to procure fancier pirate clothes, equipment, and decorations for their ships.

My friend and I set sail on a quest to find treasure. The quest had three different stages. In each we were led to an island and either given riddles to solve or a map with Xs on it. During part of the adventure, a squall kicked up and the ship was tossed about violently. Skeletons fired on us with canons from towers around the island we were trying to reach. My friend managed to get into one of the towers and defeat the skeletons with his scimitar and take control of the canon. I stayed behind, bailing water from my ship, patching holes, and trying to keep it steered in the right direction. It was all quite difficult.

We muddled through, the storm passed, and we found our treasure. Twice more we sailed to islands, dug up booty, and sailed away. As we headed home to turn in our swag, we pulled out instruments and played a lonesome Celtic tune as the sun set and our sail billowed. We were, of course, running with our lights off so as not to attract other pirates, and to let us get a jump on them if we happened across them, and so the deck was dark when the sun dipped below the waves. Once we had completed our quest, we sank our ship in the shallows and played it down with the same tune on a hurdy-gurdy and accordion. Then we said goodnight over our microphones, wished each other a blessing, and shared how much we enjoyed the time with each other. We hadn't seen each other in over eight months as careers and distance make it hard to meet in person, but we met once a week on the seas, using terms like port, starboard, windward, and leeward, as we created a story together. The game developers didn't write the story, but they made the world where we could craft one.

I will talk more about agency and some of its ethical ramifications in video games in the next chapter, but I want to emphasize here that games allow people, and this includes people in the congregations of churches, to tell fantastical stories alone and together. They foster creativity and expression in new media. They let people solve highly complex puzzles, defeat hoardes of goblins, and talk their enemies down from their wicked ways. Games like *Minecraft* let us sculpt in grass, dirt, and stone to make glorious castles or complex mine systems. Games like *The Witness* let us bang our heads against logic puzzles until we wake up the next day with a Eureka! moment. And, when we get the chance, we share these stories with each other.

Friendly Competition

I have a complex relationship with competition. My fundamental understanding of reality is that at the heart of all things is a Triune being who is the antithesis of competition. The only negatives in the Trinity are ones that indicate distinction. The Father is not the Son; the Son is not the Spirit. The three persons are interpenetrating, completely self-giving, and their distinction and unity are beyond human comprehension and expression. They are, indeed, more united because they are distinct. This is the great mystery of being and love at the root of all things.

Creation, as the limited and diverse image of this infinite plenitude of love and self-gift, should be a place of cooperation and unbounded love. All Christian expression should be an expression of charity in all things. But the world is more complex than that. The evolutionary process by which we come into being as a species is a mechanism of competition. We have competition deep within our psychology. Indeed, we find that when we set our minds to compete, we tend to accomplish far greater things than if we are merely satisfied with what we have and where we are.

This conflict between the Christian ideal of peaceable cooperation and natural competition is seen in Alfred Lord Tennyson's poem "In Memoriam A.H.H.," in which Tennyson considers the conflict between the nobility of the human spirit and the destiny of death. His departed friend is the one,

Who trusted God was love indeed
And love Creation's final law—

Tho' Nature, red in tooth and claw
With ravine, shriek'd against his creed—

The solution I find is that competition as it exists with "red in tooth and claw" may not have been the original plan for creation, but, whatever has happened to it, competition is now a reality and can be redeemed by God. Competition can be made a glory of what C. S. Lewis calls "complex good." A redeemed competition can be used by God to make us determined, loyal, brave, mutually supportive, and glorious. An unredeemed competition can lead to cheating, lying, jealousy, and hatred.

My experience of playing video games with friends, especially Christian friends, has given me many examples of redeemed competition. There is a complex joy that can be mined from the competition between friends that is lost to those who do not love their competitors. In friendly competition we find that we can glory in our opponents' victories as well as in our own. We can celebrate the amazing shot, the ingenious tactics, and the wise foresight that defeated us in the end because we don't believe the fundamental message of unredeemed competition, which is that we are playing a zero-sum game, and that your victory is my loss. Instead, redeemed play in all forms, not just video games, allows players to be like the scribes of the kingdom, bringing forth treasures old (my victory is my glory) and new (but so is yours).

This perspective on competition is not new. Christians have been playing each other in chess, rugby, soccer, football, baseball, basketball, tennis, and scores of other games for centuries. Christians tilted with each other from horseback in suits of armor, wrestled with each other, and met in the boxing ring. They have gloried in the humility of trying their very best and meeting a more capable opponent. Video games are another place where the Christian expression of redeemed competition can come to light.

Fallen Play

The picture I have drawn in this chapter is one that shows games in their best light because I believe the assumptions that surround them are often unfair. I have attempted to show how they can tell stories that deeply engage us, present worlds for us to explore, and provide us with opportunities for friendly cooperation and competition. Because my argument is that we should be taking video games seriously, I have not emphasized the troubling side. However, once the church accepts that video games have something important to contribute to our contemplation of ultimate questions and are worth considering, the church must take an honest look at the darker side of video games.

I am not thinking of those games that present stories of questionable or outright immoral behavior. Nor am I thinking of those "open" games that let a person play as an upright or low-down dirty kind of character. I have no issue with the game that lets you talk your way, shoot your way, or seduce your way out of a situation. Play is the place where we can indulge a little and have every chance of slipping past any moral consequences. All of this I will get into in the next chapter. Instead, I'm thinking of two problems with video games in general. The first is the assembly of games that are designed purely to foment a desire rooted in doing harm. The second is the community that gathers around video games. Both are areas where the church must be both aware and active in engaging the world of play.

I want to represent the collection of games that concern me with two examples; alongside them I'd like to put two counter-examples. The two games in question are *Hatred* (2015) and *RapeLay* (2006). Next to these I'd like to put the much-touted *Grand Theft Auto* series, and the once controversial, but now perhaps somewhat quaint, *Leisure Suit Larry* games.

Hatred, made by Destructive Creations, is a game in which you play a character who deeply hates the world around him and simply wants to murder as many people as he possibly can. The goal is to spread as much suffering as you can before you are gunned down by police. The graphics are dark, the people in the game other than you are only there to be the objects of your homicidal rage, and the player is encouraged not to have any empathy for them. The player fends off police by killing them; not only can the player gun down the civilian population but the player also executes them as they struggle and try to get away after they have been shot. There is, as far as I can tell, no purpose to the game other than the simulation of hatred and nihilism. The character has decided to die, and he plans to send as many people to the grave with him as he can. There is no exploration of the character's background, no attempt to contextualize the problems that might have led him to this tragic moment, and no demonstration of the cost of such a rampage to those who are affected by it. The sight of grieving loved ones, if it were it shown in the game, would likely be used to enhance the sense of accomplishment of evil.

Next to this I would like to put the series *Grand Theft Auto* (*GTA*), by Rockstar Games, and, specifically, *Grand Theft Auto V* (*GTA V*), which is, at the time of this writing, the most recent in the series. For several versions, *GTA* has been increasingly focused on stories and characters. *GTA: San Andreas* drew its characters and setting heavily from the movie *Boyz n the Hood*; *GTA: Vice City* focused on a 1980s *Miami Vice* setting; *GTA IV* was set in an analog of New York, focusing on an immigrant from a former Soviet Bloc country who wants to come to America to start over, but is pulled into the shady dealings of the underworld; *GTA V* introduces the first storyline with three protagonists.

It is worth saying that in all these games, you play as a criminal who is either trying to reform and get out of "the life" or actively pursuing a criminal career. In either case, the characters are seeking something. They care about other characters and are not wanton killers. In no *GTA* game do you play as a person whose goal is a mass-murder spree. The closest the series gets to that is a character named Trevor in *GTA V*. He is both the most amoral character the series presents, and one of the most tragic. He is introduced as he murders one of the protagonists of a previous *GTA* adventure. Trevor is morally reprehensible and generally a menace to society, but there are two significant elements that distinguish him from the character in *Hatred*.

The first is that Trevor's corruption, manipulation, and psychopathic tendencies are not recklessly glorified like the murders in *Hatred*. Trevor is complex. He has friends he cares about, even if he treats them terribly. He has been betrayed, he has a strange code of honor, and he even has a dastardly charm. Excepting his tendency to kill, I've known people like Trevor. They are people in desperate need of help, people who have been badly damaged. I saw, in his character, the possible outcome for one of the kids I grew up with, who fortunately turned away from drugs and submitted himself to baptism a few years ago. In a different version of our lives, he might have been Trevor.

The things you do as Trevor are bad, there's no getting around it. The things you do in *Grand Theft Auto* games would be, if you did them in the real world, immoral and illegal. And the things that you can do in a *GTA* game would range from the ill-advised to the monstrous. Still, the difference between *GTA* and *Hatred* is massive, at least from my perspective.

The point of *Hatred* is to feel no empathy, to have no sense of humor, simply to hate the people around you. It is, even if not so intended, a game that appears designed to live out revenge fantasies—the kind we fear some peole have before they take a real gun and cause real damage and excruciating sorrow in our world. The goal of *Hatred* is wholesale slaughter.

None of that is the point of *GTA*. *GTA* allows you to commit widespread virtual violence, but it doesn't revel in it. Instead, you can spend sixty hours in a full game of *GTA V* committing crimes—many of them involving shootouts—yet never go on a shooting spree. And, even if you do, you may have vastly different motivations than someone playing *Hatred*. My common practice when playing *GTA* is to play entirely without civilian casualties, if I can. Sometimes the cars don't handle well, and sometimes you get in a tussle with the police. None of it brings up malicious feelings in me. None of it gives me satisfaction that that innocent person, or a police officer, has gotten what they deserve. However, when I am satisfied, or bored, or tired, I will often save my progress and make use of the combat elements of the game. I will shoot it out with the ever-escalating police presence and see how long I can last. I might hunker down in a restaurant, commit a crime, and then let the police, swat teams, and, eventually, military characters of the game pour in and do my best to stay alive under the increasing danger. I derive no sadistic pleasure in seeing "people" shot. I simply like the challenge of the escalating level of difficulty, knowing that, in the end, I will fall in a hail of bullets.

There are people who go on shooting sprees in *GTA* for the same reason they might in *Hatred*. They feel hatred. They want the people in the game to stand in for the people they wish they could hurt. But *GTA* is not designed with that in mind, or at least it does not appear to be. Instead, *GTA* has a system in place that insures that if you do something flagrant, the police will respond. Alternatively, *Hatred*'s whole point is to do malicious harm to people and cause them suffering. There is nothing else to do. If you don't kill innocents and police, you've played the game badly. In *GTA* you can play "robber" as you might in a game of "cops and robbers." In *Hatred*, there is only the titular emotion.

Now, turning from violence to sex, the other, somehow larger taboo when it comes to our culture, we find the game *RapeLay*, made by Illusion Games. As you might glean from the title, it's a game about nonconsensual sex. The game is a collection of small vignettes in which you manipulate a disembodied hand to grope and prod at the members of a family of women so that you can take them against their will. There isn't much more to the game. It is a simulator that treats women as play things. It has no other point. There is no character, no real story, no empathy.

Comparatively, the *Leisure Suit Larry* games, made famous in the eighties for their smutty content, tell the stories of the kind of guy you might see at a bar on Friday night and wonder, "What on earth is he thinking?" Larry is on a quest for sex. However, as Rachel Presser has argued,[1] despite the outrage that often follows the game, the *Larry* games emphasize the need for consent, the ability to good-naturedly accept rejection, and the superiority of emotional connection to simple physical interaction.

Even so, the game is prurient, it's immature, and it's largely played for laughs. Larry is a schlub and the women around him know he's a schlub. Their rejections of him are humorous, but there is no hint that Larry is trying to bed them to get revenge. Larry has a sense of humor about it all too. There is, of course, the problematic way in which the games present the pursuit of sex—not as the culmination of a loving relationship, nor always even as something people do for mutual enjoyment, but as a kind of secret treasure the women possess that men must figure out how to unlock. *Larry*, of course,

---

1. Rachel Presser, "The Surprising Feminist Overtures of a Leisure Suit Larry Retrospective," Medium, September 10, 2018, https://medium.com/mammon-machine-zeal/the-surprising-feminist-overtures-of-a-leisure-suit-larry-retrospective-f8b5950c29f1

needs serious critiquing, especially around the idea that sex = victory. But, since it is played for laughs, there is a certain amount of critique in Larry's understanding of sex inherent in the game already. Far from excusing his antics with a "boys will be boys" attitude, the games treat Larry as the butt of the joke, while at the same time allowing his constant optimism to allow players to still feel for him and root for him.

Some may find any sexual content in books, movies, television shows, or music to be in bad taste. They will see Larry's escapades, even when their problematic elements have been addressed, simply as smut. I must simply disagree, and so does a significant portion of Christian cultural history. There is an equally long history of bawdy humor in Christian culture as there is of military entertainment. If one embraces that the soldierly and the sultry can be subjects of Christian entertainment, then the difference between *Larry* and *RapeLay* matters. *Larry* needs critiquing, and perhaps can receive it in the games themselves. *RapeLay* is no more than an exercise in virtually enacting sexual assault.

There are many games like *Hatred* and *RapeLay*. There are games where the point is to shoot Muslims, to shoot students in schools, and to manipulate events to sleep with women, with or without their consent. These are all problematic, but there may be an upside to them that demonstrates why it is so important that our churches are conversant in the games people are playing. If someone plays *Hatred* and enjoys it, they may just have a darker sense of humor, but they may also be finding a desired simulation of things that they feel drawn to do. If we know the games and we can talk to our congregations about them, and engage them in shame-free conversation about why they enjoy what they play, then we can gain insight and offer help where it is needed.

This brings me to the second major dark sector: gaming communities. There are a multitude of healthy, happy, friendly, encouraging gaming communities in the world. At my own church, we have a game night on Saturdays where we invite people, as part of a meetup group, to come into the rectory and play board games or role-play games. For a few hours every week, a group of fifteen to twenty people sit around tables, slay goblins, cast spells, buy up properties, assign workers, roll dice, and do all the things that people do in games. It's a friendly group. It's not perfect. There have been a few tense moments here and there. But, overall, it is growing into a group, not just of people that play together, but of friends who care for each other. This is the ideal: people coming together through the love of play and building human bonds.

But there are sectors of the video-gaming community that do not work this way. Instead, largely fueled by the anonymity of the internet, they are a thriving expression of the sexism, racism, homophobia, and transphobia that gather around gaming. The use of racial and sexual slurs on voice chat in many online games is well known. Many people turn off their voice-chat features or reserve those features for people they already know in real life.

A good example of both the need for critique as well as the toxicity around that critique is the "Gamergate" phenomenon that dominated public video game discussions in 2014. Elements of the online gaming community came together to harass women in the gaming community that they saw as either dishonest or dangerous to the continuation of gaming as it existed. Women like Zoe Quinn, Brianna Wu, and Anita Sarkeesian received harassing messages and threats against them and their families. Threats of rape and murder were leveled against these and other women in the larger community of gaming, either for, as the Gamergaters saw it, unfairly using their sexuality to promote their games, or critiquing a male-dominated industry that often treats women with shocking unfairness in the games that it makes and plays.

In both the Gamergate and online gaming sides of deeply problematic behavior, both anonymity and fame play important parts. People who feel that they can harm others by exposing their home addresses to the public— an act known as "doxing"—tend to do so without being willing to present their own information. There are more examples of the destructive nature of the community around video games. Of course, there are similar examples in the communities around sports and politics. There has not been, to my knowledge, a single riot-related death of anyone associated with video games, though professional sports cannot say the same. This is not to say that sports are somehow worse than games, but to say that human communities will always be laced with fallenness. This fallenness can be kept, to some degree, in check by a healthy openness in our activities. When we can operate entirely in the shadows, when we can say whatever we feel without anyone being able to call us out for it, or threaten things just to scare another person without being confronted, the angels of our worst natures seem to come flapping into view. The church must address all of this, not by standing outside of the gaming community and wagging a parental finger, but by standing within it and engaging it constructively and compassionately.

Conclusion

Leaders of faith communities need to have a level head when it comes to dealing with video games. The presence of problematic, sometimes deeply problematic, elements in the hobby of gaming should not blind anyone to the artistic, narrative, imaginative, aesthetic, intellectual, and social good of video games. Instead, we must be realistic and aware about this activity that millions of people around the world are engaging in every day. To shun it, to be willfully unaware of it, or, worse, to dismiss it, is irresponsible and robs us of the ability both to communicate with those who are members or potential members of our parishes, and to address the issues that exist for them.

I cannot say for sure, but I feel confident that if the members of Gamergate had sat down with their local parish priest or minister and discussed their ethical concerns, that the character of that discussion would have been very different. A Christian perspective on charity, about praying for and loving one's enemies, and perhaps, given the right setting, a discussion of *jus in bello*, specifically, of the Christian idea of proportionality would have been useful.

Having made a case for both the good of gaming and displaying some of what I see as its deep flaws, I will turn once more to the issue of violence in video games as well as the question of ethics.

VIOLENCE

THE VIRTUAL AND THE REAL

Just after I graduated college with a BA in biblical studies, I did what many young people with a liberal arts degree do: I got a job in an industry entirely unrelated to what I had studied for four years. I became the manager of a hobby store, which, though it wasn't biblically related and paid very little, was a great job. In my short tenure selling model tanks, electric trains, remote control cars, and role-play game books, I encountered many strains of geekdom that were new to me.

It wasn't that I was unfamiliar with geek culture in general. In fact, I was very familiar with the geeky trappings of my youth: *Star Wars*, Saturday morning cartoons, and comic books. I still have my *Star Wars* action figures that I got from my parents and grandparents stashed in a container somewhere. I retain a fondness for the *Teenage Mutant Ninja Turtles*. But there was one kind of geekdom I knew better than the rest: comic books.

I knew comic book geekdom well; I even sent a letter to *Green Lantern* comics to name the magazine's letter column. To my fourteen-year-old surprise, they picked it and, for something like nine glorious issues, the letter column was called "Batteries Not Included." Then, of course, Hal Jordan, the main Green Lantern for the previous forty-odd years left the comic and was replaced by an upstart. I don't think I've ever forgiven Kyle Rayner for voiding my letter column name.

In addition to comics, I loved role-play games and sometimes played with my brother and his friends. Mostly, however, I sat in my room by myself, created characters, and tried to play adventures with them. Though I hadn't met many people who loved them the way I did until many years later, I also loved video games. I even wrote a text adventure in my sophomore year of college called "Deephome." I was well versed in the world of being a geek. I loved the things that didn't make me cool, though I had rarely encountered anyone who loved the things I loved.

Given how much of a geek I was, I was in no position, I thought, to judge anyone for their unpopular obsessions. That all changed when I was running the hobby store. During the heady days of *D&D 3.0*, a guy in his early twenties came in to buy a *Dungeons & Dragons* book and started talking about one of his adventures. He explained how he had gone down into hell (or Hades) to get Thor's hammer, Mjolnir, and how he hefted the hammer in his hand, and held the weapon forged by the dwarves Sindri and Brokkr.

As he told his tale, I thought, "What a dork!" He hadn't held Mjolnir in his hand. He hadn't gone down into hell to get it. He had pretended. That's all. I liked pretending too. I had enjoyed many adventures based entirely in the imagination and the rules of the games spelled out in sourcebooks. But I hadn't done those things, the characters had. Still, his story stayed with me. As I thought more about the relationship of fantasy worlds to our own, especially virtual ones created by human beings, I began to consider questions of agency and the difference between what we do in the real world and what we do in virtual worlds. What is the difference between what I do here, at my desk at Saint Joseph's University, and what I do when I'm playing a game like *The Witcher*? Indeed, what is the difference between what I do when I read *The Witcher* books by Andrzej Sapkowski and when I play the games based on those books?

It's clear that there is a difference between my world, the world of a game, and the world of a book. In fact, the difference is so stark that one might ask why anyone needs to point it out. The reality is that people who play games feel connected to the things they do in those games. They feel connected to many of the characters they play. Sometimes they feel as if the characters merely stand in for them, like in games such as the *Fallout* or the *Skyrim* series where a player has total control over a character's appearance, skills, and personality. Other times, they feel as if they are participating in an existing character's story in a strange, or even mysterious way, such as with Max or Chloe from the *Life Is Strange* series, Marcus from *Watch Dogs 2*, or Wei Shen from *Sleeping Dogs*.

The virtual world bleeds over into the real. The characters, stories, and challenges that we meet in a game stay with us. While driving, falling asleep, or sitting in church in the real world, we think about puzzles, about how to shave time off a driving course, and about the choices we make in games. Of course, the real world bleeds into our gaming in the form of conversation during a multiplayer game, or through our moods. Anger makes us less accurate in a puzzle game, fatigue slows our reactions, and a well-rested mind figures out a riddle quicker than a tired one.

These two worlds bleed into each other so much that I have encountered academics who insist there is no difference between the two. This book is an affirmation that the line between the two worlds is fuzzy but real. This chapter is an attempt to articulate my perspective on that fuzzy line. To do so, I want to use an idea that comes up in most introduction to philosophy courses. It has been around for about twenty-three hundred years, and has been a major influence on Western philosophy and religions. This philosophical tool was proposed by the Greek philosopher Plato. Broadly speaking, he conceived of two kinds of worlds: the world of ideas, and the world of things. He was trying to solve the relationship between the universal and the particular, one of the perennial problems of philosophy. He taught concerning the relationship between categories that similar things fit into (for example, animals) and the things that fit into the category (a particular horse).

When we think about these two categories, questions start to pop up. What makes a horse an animal? Are all horses animals? What makes all horses alike? More to the point, are the similarities between horses just in our minds (meaning that they are just descriptions that we make up), or is the connection between horses transcendent, existing beyond the natural world? Is there a "horsiness" that all horses participate in, or is that just a category in our brains?

The relationship between the universal and the particular raises a host of other questions, but for the moment these will suffice. Different philosophers have answered these questions in various ways, but Plato said that the group that encompasses all of these different things was very real. He believed this to be true of all things. All trees had a common reality that bound them together. All fish were bound by a "fishness" that made them different from trees. Yet both groups were a part of a larger reality that bound them all together and distinguished them from rocks or air.

Plato's theory was called the Theory of the Forms, or Ideas. He believed that there was a world above our own where the ideas existed in pure form. That world was more real than our own because it was unchanging and everlasting. Our existing world, transient and chaotic, was only a pale comparison with that realer world. His idea was demonstrated in the famous "myth of the cave" from his *Republic*. The people in the cave were bound to one wall and watched shadows march across the opposite cave wall. One man (Socrates) was freed from his bonds and stood up to see that there was a great fire in front of which the images of trees, birds, and mountains were held up. He thought the images must be the real world, but he had been looking at shadows the whole time. But that was not the end of his story. He found a hole in the cave wall and climbed up toward it. The climb was difficult and painful, but he endured and emerged from the cave where he saw real trees, real sun, and real mountains. He had finally seen the real world of which the world of shadows were only a thin imitation.

C. S. Lewis took up the myth in the last book of the *Chronicles of Narnia* series, in which the Narnia that we have all known and loved was ended by Aslan and the "true" Narnia was made anew. The old Narnia was compared to a dream and the new to reality. The old Narnia was the "shadowlands" of the new, real world. Lewis was criticized by some for his reliance on Plato, and perhaps those criticisms have merit. But the idea of two worlds existing together is indispensable for Christianity, even though, at times, it can be applied in unhelpful ways. It helps to clarify the ideas that God is eternal and more real than the created world, that God exists by God's own virtue of existence, and that the world exists because God has commanded it to exist. Our world is dependent on God, and, therefore, less real. Our world, a collection of particular and limited things, is an image of the infinite One God. All that we have rests on God; even qualities like unity and diversity find their ultimate origin in God's own oneness and threeness.

I am going to leave behind many of the particulars of Platonic philosophy and steal the idea of a hierarchy of existence in which God is the highest and most fundamental reality. God is the highest existence that all other realities depend on; God depends on nothing. The orthodox teaching of Christianity for millennia has been that God would exist as God is without us. While there are some difficulties with this view (what about the Incarnation?), it points us in the right direction toward understanding that God's reality is more fundamental and robust than our own. C. S. Lewis depicts this difference in *The Great Divorce*. The people from hell who visit heaven are insubstantial ghosts; their feet can't even bend the grass of heaven. The people of heaven, on the other hand, are so real and solid that they can't make themselves small enough to get down into hell. The same idea appears in the last book of the Narnia series as the children chase Aslan "higher up and higher in" to the remade Narnia. The more the heavenly people are like God, the more real they are. The further into the new Narnia the children run, the more real they find the world.

Before video games existed, we had an inkling of the fact that fantasy wasn't entirely devoid of existence. Fictional characters in books are real to us and they have some semblance of reality. One finds this in the dialogue between Old Scrooge and the Ghost of Christmas Past in the George C. Scott version of *A Christmas Carol*. When they look at the young Ebenezer, solitary as the term ends, the ghost considers that the boy is alone, but Scrooge disagrees, saying, "He has his friends, even on this day—from his beloved books. His Ali Baba, dear old honest Ali Baba. And the Sultan's groom, turned upside down by the Genie."

The ghost replies, "But not a real child to talk to, not a living person."

Scrooge is unimpressed. "Robinson Crusoe, not real? And Friday? And the parrot with the green body and yellow tail? Not real?" He laughs because they are real, just not real in the same way we are.

We lend fictional characters their reality and grant them a share in our own existence. The lower reality, which on its own is merely ink on a page or a voice in a recording, is granted a greater reality when the world that is higher and more real participates in it. This echoes Christian theology rooted in the school of Alexandria from the third century onward. God, who makes our world out of nothingness, shares God's own being with our world so that it might be grounded in the Divine Reality. It is what the Fathers of the church called the "happy exchange." God takes on a created nature to share God's uncreated nature with us. Or, as Irenaeus put it succinctly, "God became human, so that humans could become God."

This hierarchy of existence is one that I find especially helpful when dealing with the question of our relationship to video games. This is partially because the hierarchy of existence makes sense when we think about video games having an existence, but not the same kind of existence as our world. Mostly I find it useful because if we take this perspective, the idea of the worlds we create slips easily into the hierarchy one level down from our own: God at the top, our world below and less real than God, and virtual worlds—or even all imaginary worlds—below our world and God. Further, it allows us to explore, much like J. R. R. Tolkien, the idea that we are creating something in a way that expresses our identities as the image of God. God creates, so do we. Our creating is a little picture of God's grand creation.

What is new and unique about video games and virtual worlds in general is that they have a kind of existence outside of our minds. They do not exist the same as marks on a page that have no reality until we pick them up, read them, and let them become in fantastical worlds in our minds. Instead, Azeroth is actually out there, waiting for me to log in. The world of *Zork* and its Great Underground Empire exists right now on someone's computer. Indeed, it could be running on mine while I write these words, waiting for me to interact. A video game's internal fictional reality is more robust than that of written, recorded, or filmed fiction. It is a thing we can join, change, and interact with in myriad ways. But, as far as reality goes, it is still one level down from our world.

Theological Problems

From a Christian perspective the virtual world presents us with many interesting intellectual problems. What are we to think of the actions of gamers in their game worlds? Is playing games a worthwhile pursuit for Christians? Can we use virtual spaces for worship? Does the virtual/real divide help us think more clearly about God's relationship to creation?

In one way or another, this book, as a whole, attempts to address all of these questions, at least briefly. In this chapter, however, I'd like to apply the lens I have described so far to look at a most pressing question: what about the violence? Usually, when people ask this question, they are asking it about games like *Call of Duty* or *Grand Theft Auto*, which are games where, depending on how you play, you might be responsible for the virtual deaths of hundreds or thousands of "people." Surely this ability to do virtual evil is a problem. Further, given how violent games often are, is it appropriate to talk about them in the same breath as the Incarnation, for example?

I had a brief conversation a couple of years back with a prominent scholar in the field of video games and religion. When I brought up violence and the Incarnation, she insisted that she didn't want Jesus to have anything to do with virtual violence. Personally, I'm not so sure that I agree with her. To approach this problem, I would like to start with the premise that there are three levels of reality that concern us. I think that there are likely more, and some might argue there are fewer. At the top level is God, in the middle is our reality, and at the bottom is a game of *Grand Theft Auto V* (*GTA V*), which, as of this writing, is the most profitable entertainment property in history. From the Christian perspective, that top level, God, is unchangeably and unadulteratedly good. Indeed, God, as the source of all goodness, is Goodness. This top level of reality, which Christianity affirms as the Triune God, has no space for evil, and no possibility of it. In 1 John 1:5, the author says, "This is the message we have heard from him and proclaim to you, that God is light and in him there is no darkness at all." George MacDonald, the great nineteenth-century author and preacher, said that we must never attribute evil to God. If the Bible, or a theologian, or a preacher assigns evil to God, even if they then slap the label of "goodness" on the action, we must not believe it about God. Indeed, MacDonald insisted that we "cannot think too well of God." As far as the top level of reality goes, no evil at all can take place. It is a realm of pure goodness.

Our own realm, the order of creation, is a universe in which both good and evil exist. We maintain the inherently good character of all of creation, but one need not look far to find that good creation being used by human beings for all manner of evil. Indeed, we need not look far at all. We have done it. Both the author and the reader of this book have done it. We participate in the use of the good world for evil.

Now, we must observe that this evil that we do in our world does not infect the reality one step up. God is neither physically harmed, nor corrupted by our selfish, spiteful, and generally nasty behavior. For God to be hurt by these things, God must enter into our level of reality. The fourth-century church father Athanasius observed that it was precisely for this reason, to confront our pain, sorrow, and our death, that God took on flesh. From Athanasius's perspective, the Second Person of the Trinity descended into our level of reality to bring it back up to God. This is the "happy exchange" mentioned earlier.

In our last level of reality, *GTA V*, we find a world that looks like our own. There are objects that look like cars, roads, buildings, planes, water, trees, rocks, and people. There are also plenty of weapons that can mow down the "people" in a way that mimics genuinely horrific and tragic actions in our own world. Around America, at least, news broadcasts have pointed out that a player in the *GTA* series could pick up a prostitute, drive her to a secluded place, have sex, and then run her over and take her money. It's all quite disgusting. Or, it would be if it were real. And, indeed, the more the graphics imitate our reality, the more real the situation appears to us. It can bring actual events to mind. But here is the big question: Are these acts immoral if they are contained within the video game? Are they, in any way, the occasions for moral choice in a similar way to those same actions in real life?

To answer, we must first ask what makes an act immoral in our own world. There are a lot of different answers to this question, but they either come down to a viewpoint that says that immoral acts are objectively immoral, or they are merely strong cultural preferences. In other words, the question of morality comes down either to the fact that killing a five-year-old child is genuinely, always, and everywhere wrong, and that any culture, group, or person anywhere and at any time can say to someone else "you are wrong for wanting to kill that child," or we simply have a very strong cultural preference that five-year-olds shouldn't be killed. We can say to another culture or group "you are wrong for wanting to kill that child," but what we really are saying is, "We very strongly would prefer if you didn't kill that child, but ultimately it is a matter of your preference versus ours." In this second instance, no one can be genuinely right or wrong about morality; one can only make arguments for why a particular morality is more useful, more expedient, or less damaging than another.

Christianity falls strongly on the side of the first position. It insists that some actions and viewpoints are genuinely good, and some are genuinely bad. This does not mean that every circumstance for decision-making is just black and white; the world is awash in grays. But the church maintains that in all instances it is always morally wrong to kill children, it is always wrong to sexually assault another person, and, ultimately, it is always wrong to hate another human being. There are, of course, more acts that fall into the category of being simply right or wrong, but many of these other questions are more complex, requiring situational considerations. There is, of course, significant debate between the Roman Catholic Church and many Protestant denominations about the morality of abortion or euthanasia. There is further debate about who has the right to marry and what constitutes sexual immorality. In the context of Christian theology, these debates do not usually take place from the perspective of what is most useful or beneficial, but are instead concerned with genuine issues of right and wrong, virtue and sin.

If we side with Christianity to say that there are genuinely good and bad actions, we must ask why these actions are good or bad. One important tradition of Christian morality is that creation has objective value. It can only be objectively wrong to harm someone or something if, in fact, that person or object has objective value. It is also objectivey right to defend those who are powerless. Thus, it is always wrong to harm or kill children because, first, children are objectively valuable because they are people, and, second, because they are always objectively deserving of our protection.

Value is always hierarchical. Gold is valuable, not because it is inherently valuable, but because humans value both beauty and rarity. If we did not value these two qualities, gold would not have any kind of value. An old raggedy stuffed rabbit with one eye missing and its stitching bursting around its belly is inherently without value, but to the child who clings to it and loves it, it takes on value.

One need not believe in God to understand that value works on a hierarchical level. However, without God, it seems impossible to come up with anything like objective value in the universe. Our world is merely a wild, sometimes lovely, sometimes merciless dance of energy. Human beings are inextricably part of that dance. We are not above it, no matter how much we would like to be. If humans have any value in such a system, it is the value of a part of a whole. But one must ask where the whole gets its value. If there is no being above it to give it value, then where does that value come from? Consequently, where does the value of the people in it come from? In a world where no God exists, there may be value, but it must remain subjective and, ultimately, a preference. And, thus, all morality remains a preference as its hierarchy remains relative.

Alternatively, if there is an eternal being who is the foundation of all existence, love, and reason, then that being can imbue the world with value and can say authoritatively, "Humans are valuable, and you should not lie to them, murder them, take what is theirs, betray them, or, ultimately, worship them." Without God, we might say, "I prefer not to do those things, and I think everyone would be happier if we didn't do those things," but we would only be talking about a preference. Perhaps it is a perfectly reasonable preference, but it is not one that holds any authority when another person replies, "That's nice, but I prefer to take what you have and kill you." A person who believes in God can say without logical contradiction, "You would be doing evil if you did." Whether this would be effective depends entirely on the person they are talking to. But I am more concerned with the logic of the thing, and the logic here is that the world can only have objective value when it is given that value by something above it.

Another example may be helpful. Imagine a classroom in which the students decide to give each other grades. They might each give each other all sorts of grades, but these grades are ultimately meaningless. They might prefer some grades over others, probably the ones that are higher, that benefit them, and make them feel good, but all the grades are ultimately worthless. However, the grade the professor gives them is valuable because the professor, for at least the purpose of evaluation, is above the students. The teacher gives the grade genuine value because, above the teacher is an institution that values the teacher's ability to grade students. Not just any teacher can grade this class, only the one imbued with value. A step up, the state imbues the institution with value so that its grades and professors matter in the larger context of society through accreditation. And the chain continues. Value is imbued from the outside.

We could respond that people give each other value and that there is no hierarchy there. That is true, but the value that we give each other is either personal (I value someone, but that doesn't mean anyone else should), or corporate (we all value each other). In either case, the value given in those situations fails to stand up to scrutiny, however, when someone comes along and says, "But I don't value this person, or your group opinion." At that point, we are at an impasse because what makes my valuing of a person more important or better founded than someone else's failure to value them? In a group situation, what makes one group's values more important than another's? For things to have genuine value at one level of being, they must be given that value from a higher level of being.

With that position in place, we find that the actions we perform are moral or immoral because we do them to beings that have value. If you kill me, it is immoral because I am valuable as a person. If I say something to you that I should not say, if I betray your trust, if I misuse my power, then I do evil, because you are a valuable person. When I have done evil in the past, it is not because I have broken some arbitrary law, but because I have committed offenses against valuable people.

We must add to this that no one on the same level of being is genuinely above another person on that level of being; that is, no one is more valuable than another. There is no one on our level of being who can remove the value of another. Even Christ, who taught with divine authority, taught as a human the same value that God imbues the world with. He did not override human value by human authority; indeed, he imbued humans with an even greater value by his life, death, and resurrection. With all of that said, we can now consider why, from my perspective, the violent acts in video games are not immoral. Or at least, they are not as long as they do not fall into one of two very particular sets of circumstances.

When we think about the actions in a game of *GTA V* from this hierarchical perspective, we find that the actions between objects in a computer simulation can only have the kind of value that is inherent to that level of existence. To understand that level of existence, we must consider that there are three layers of being for any computer program. The first is the physical organization of matter and energy in our world, which is the computer hardware and the electricity running through it, which is nothing more than moving very small parts of our world around. Computers are not special when it comes to the laws of physics. They aren't doing something new. They follow the same fundamental physical laws that everything else does. A computer is simply an arrangement of matter and energy in a way that takes advantage of these laws to produce results that are advantageous to us. The things that happen in video games are mainly the rearrangement of electrons in the tiny capacitors of computer memory. And given that there is no value given to these arrangements either by us or God, we can safely say that nothing immoral happens when we do anything at all in a video game, at least on this layer.

The second layer of a video game is the collection of abstractions based on the physical relationships of capacitors and computational elements in the computer. This is generally what we call the "program" itself. In the program there are "objects" that interact with each other based on a set of rules. The Player Object has certain characteristics and so does the Pedestrian Object. At this level of the computer program there is no similarity whatsoever between the Player Object and a human being. The same is true of the Pedestrian Object. They are nothing like the things they represent to us when we play the game. They do not have value. They are created and destroyed without moral action when we turn a game off and on. Turning off a video game is by no means an immoral act—unless it falls under the very specific set of circumstances that I will address below.

Finally, there is the sensory information that come to us from whatever devices we are using to play the game. Primarily these stimuli are images and sounds, though they can be tactile as well. It is here that the organization of our material world, translated through the abstractions of the program, turns into something that may look like our world. That specific organization of electrons in computer memory that is presented on a screen as a man walking down this street in *GTA V* appears to us as a person. We then have a choice as to whether we will ignore or harm them. But, even here, though these images look like people, they have no value. They are not the same as people in our world; even at the level of artistic representation they do not have the value of the beings they represent. In other words, a picture of a person is not more valuable than a picture of a rock because they represent things that have different values in the real world. A picture has more value because it is better art, or because someone loves it, but it would be ridiculous to say that a bad and blurry picture of someone turning away from the camera is somehow more valuable than Da Vinci's earliest known art or a landscape by Santa Maria Della Neve just because people are more important than buildings.

It is further problematic to say that violence done against representations of people is itself immoral. If it were, much of human art would be immoral. Indeed, Hamlet would be a deeply immoral play since so much violence happens to depictions of human beings.

Beyond this kind of argument from tradition, we must perceive that there is no logical ground for arguing that virtual representations of people have any value in themselves. Again, they may be materially valuable as art, but they carry no intrinsic value that would make virtual violence against them immoral.

We, as players who come from the world above the virtual, perform actions in virtual worlds that have no moral value. And this must extend to all of the actions, no matter how distasteful they appear to us because of their similarity to our real world. Thus, at least from this perspective, violence in video games cannot be immoral.

Exceptions to the Rule

As I mentioned above, there are two very particular sets of circumstances in which human actions in virtual worlds can be immoral. The first is when a person does not think they are interacting with a virtual world, but instead intends harm against the real world. The second is when human action in the virtual rises from the virtual back to the real to inflict moral evil on the real world.

Regarding the first situation, a human action can be immoral because the human attempts to do evil against the real world but simply misses its target. This could happen for several reasons, but we can most easily imagine it in a situation in which a simulation created by a computer is so convincing that a person does not know that they are interacting with a computer. This could be a visual and tactile simulation, but it could also be as simple as an online chat with a computer program designed to mimic a human conversational partner. In this latter case, any attempt to cause that conversational partner emotional harm, to deceive it, or to convince it to do moral evil is itself morally wrong. This is not because the computer program itself has any value, but because moral evil is rooted in the human will to do evil. In this circumstance, the will of the person is turned to harm, deception, or temptation. The person intends to do harm. There may not be any practical harm done because the computer program cannot suffer, but there is moral evil in the person's choice to do harm.

The second circumstance is the more prevalent. In this situation, a person may simply use the virtual as a medium to enact moral evil in the real world, or may use the virtual to facilitate other moral evils in the world. It must be noted that if the virtual is merely a medium of evil, then it is no different from a telephone, from mail, or from any other tool that we use to communicate evil. If the virtual is used to facilitate other moral evils, as it might if a person practices a school shooting in a video game that enables them to do so in real life, then the video game is merely a tool of preparation like any other tool, such as a book or a shooting range, might be.

Another way of looking at these exceptions is to say that as long as an action remains at the level of the virtual—as long as an action stays within the game world, even if it resembles an act that would be evil in our world—it is without moral value. If that action ascends back up to our world and communicates moral evil, then it is immoral.

All of this can be a little complicated, so let's consider an example. Let's say that I'm playing a game of *Battlefield* with my good friend Rob. We are on opposite teams and thus trying to "kill" each other and each other's teammates. He uses a sniper-rifle and picks me off as I duck under cover trying to help one of my teammates. He shouts across the headsets that he got me, and I, looking at the shot in the replay, think, "That was a hell of a shot!" I congratulate him and curse him at the same time in a good-natured way. In all of this, we both do well. He is under no moral obligation not to shoot me; indeed, it would be suspect if he held back since we are competing against each other for the fun of it. I, being his friend, can appreciate the skill and difficulty of his shot and, in the spirit of competition, give him a verbal lashing and congratulations. All is right in the world. My character is not harmed because no real harm can come to a virtual character any more than we harm numbers by adding or subtracting from them, and nothing like an actual sniper shot that ends a real human life has taken place. However, even if we are playing on the same team, and working well together to solve puzzles in a nonviolent game, I might commit moral evil against him in the world by deceiving him, if deception isn't one of the agreed upon rules of the game. I might lie, verbally abusive him, or attempt to hurt him in some way that affects him as a person. I might do this in voice chat, or through actions in the game. I could put a block somewhere that he can't find when I know he's having a bad day. I could finish the puzzle he is working hard to complete that would deprive him of a small personal victory. My actions, which then rise to the level of my own reality, become immoral even though there is nothing inherently immoral about moving a block in my own world, let alone in a virtual world.

Cocreators of Evil

We might acknowledge that the above argument is valid, but we might also object that video games offer a distinct way of creating narratives that are ethically suspicious. Okay, we may say, virtual imitations of humans are not humans, so we can't do them harm. They can't be the objects of unethical acts. But what about the fact that by playing some of these games, people are helping to create unethical narratives? In other words, when we play a game, aren't we writing our own version of the story? Aren't we possibly creating a story in which a person does something immoral, as well as finding pleasure in creating those narratives? Isn't there something to be said against promoting the creation of unethical narratives for our pleasure and amusement?

I think this question is a matter of taste, not ethics. I don't believe that the people who write stories where the bad guy rampages through the western town and then outdraws the sheriff and gets away are culpable for creating unethical works of art. I don't think that art should reflect how we would like the world to be all of the time. I don't think that the stories we tell should always have happy endings, or, if they do, that they need to have ethical people as their central characters. When it comes down to it, complex characters and antiheroes are often the most interesting protagonists.

When it comes to taste, you may prefer stories where the bad guy doesn't do anything particularly bad. You may prefer that the hero is always ethically unimpeachable. No one can fault you for your tastes, but, on the other hand, most of the greatest human literature involves flawed heroes. From Noah to Moses to King David to Peter, heroes of the Bible committed shameful acts. Achilles and Percival, not to mention Lancelot, had deep character flaws. We could go on by listing most of Shakespeare's main characters, and the great heroes of popular fiction from Sherlock Holmes to Harry Potter. Even Christian from *The Pilgrim's Progress* made grave errors. Each chose, at some point, to do the wrong thing, to greater and lesser degrees. We might choose to bundle these stories up and put them away as bad examples of the kind of narratives we want for ourselves, but the reality is that perfect heroes are often boring.

Take Tom Clancy's Jack Ryan, for example. The character is, from my point of view, Clancy's ideal American. He served in the military, he is Catholic, and he lives a life of civic service after his military experience. The difficulty with Jack is that he always does the right thing. Clancy built tension by pitting Ryan against greater and greater difficulties, but there's little question about whether he'll do the right thing. While I think the Jack Ryan books are fine and I have enjoyed a few of them, I don't find the character particularly compelling. I don't see myself in him.

Sometimes it is good to not only read stories about dastardly doings, but to tell them ourselves. From all I can tell, Stephen King is a devoted, conscientious, down-to-earth husband and father. He's a human being with flaws, and if you read any of his autobiographical stuff, he'll tell you what they are. His horror writing is chilling, and his imagination is dark. And the last sentence doesn't negate the three above it, nor do the millions of people who have read his stories end up going out and smashing people's knees, dressing up as clowns to murder children, or opening up curio shops in order to sow dissension in small New England towns. But—and here's the kicker—it's a thrill to read his stuff.

It is a thrill to tell stories in video games where we blow up a whole city with a latent atomic bomb, or fight off the police for fifteen minutes, or wipe out the alien population of a small world. It's a thrill to take a portal down into hell and then to give the demons there, well, hell. It's a thrill to tell those stories, just like it's a thrill to talk about the time that you were an infected mimic in the board game *The Thing* and you tricked the humans into letting you on the helicopter at the end so you could infect the whole human race. It's a thrill because nothing is at stake except telling a good story and watching stuff blow up "real good."

Maybe you don't like explosions, or hoardes of zombies, or running down the street fighting off SWAT teams. Many people do. Many good people who would do whatever is in their power to help someone who is in need, who would never turn a firearm on another person, and who believe that the only way of rising from the grave is when the Lord returns in glorious loving power to judge all and gather our bodies from the ashes, get a real kick out of it. And they aren't the worse for it.

The Cause of Violence?

You may have noticed that I did not list among the ways that video games can be immoral that pesky circumstance that we all know and fear: the angry teenager who plays video games, learns to be violent, and then goes out into the world and hurts people. There's a good reason I haven't, and that is because rigorous studies have shown that there is no link between playing video games that virtually depict violence and the actual performance of violence in real life.[2] There is research that shows that consuming media that has violence can increase the chance that a person will respond to others with aggressive emotions, but that is true across all forms of media, not just video games.

So many people have grown up playing violent video games that if there was a strong link between video games and violent behavior, the numbers for violent behavior in the world have continued to increase. There is no such phenomenon. Instead, what really happens is that a lot of people play games like *Call of Duty*, *Battlefield*, and *Grand Theft Auto* and then go out from their homes to be kind, considerate, and generous people who never connect the imaginary people in the game with the real people they see around them. Their actions in the virtual never rise to the level of the real, nor does the part of the brain that decides that it's going to go on a shooting spree in a virtual city just to see how long they can last against the cops ever think for an instant that it should even attempt to punch the store clerk that is making life difficult. People know the difference between fantasy and reality.

---

2. See, for example, two recent studies, the first by a mental health PhD student who identifies as "Platinum," "Youth Violence and Video Games: A Data Analysis," Psychology and Video Games, September 13, 2018, http://platinumparagon.info/gaming-and-violence-study/?fbclid=IwAR02MnOC 3b5Hx_AfRIusBkwuIy2WZrhT6HwzyXOD0GBi3BCUf5VzMhlfO4U, and one led by Professor Andrew Przybylski, associate professor and senior research fellow and director of research at the Oxford Internet Institute: Andrew K. Przybylski and Netta Weinstein, "Violent Video Game Engagement Is Not Associated with Adolescents' Aggressive Behavior: Evidence from a Register Report," Royal Society Publishing, February 13, 2019, https://royalsocietypublishing.org/doi/10.1098/rsos.171474.

Further Considerations

While it's true that research has shown no connection between violent video games and real-life violent behavior, the fact that voice chat in video games is rife with racism and sexism is also well documented. It is here, in the verbal abuse, the intentional demeaning of other players, and the use of video games to create harm in the real world, especially around the deeply problematic and illegal activity of "swatting" in which a person maliciously calls the police to another person's house with a false report that there is violent or otherwise illegal behavior taking place there, that the real moral problems of video games exist. Further, it is in the questionable representations of races, genders, and social groups that video games join other forms of media in being the objects of moral scrutiny. It is when these games use violence to reinforce harmful stereotypes that a good case can be made for the violence in games being immoral.

But the strong divide between the virtual and the real, as it pertains to the question of objective value, shows that any actions that we perform in a video game remain without moral character as long as we know that we are doing them to beings or objects that are not real and we don't use them to try to do actual evil in our own world. In other words, unless you harm the real world, or intend to, you can't do moral evil in a video game. This perception of a strong divide between the virtual and the real will help us to consider further the questions of video games in our following chapters.

THE CHURCH'S SUSPICIONS ABOUT VIDEO GAMES

Human beings are cultural creatures. We exist and function within the freedoms and limitations of culture. We grow, mature, and readily judge the world from the perspective of our cultural assumptions. Culture not only colors how we see the world, but it also enables us to see the world. It allows us to make sense of and to categorize the things that we see. Except for the theoretical child raised by wolves, there are no humans who are not affected by some kind of culture.

Cultures do not always adapt well to new ideas. They often struggle with them, slowly integrating them, if at all, into their own warp and weft. The often-tumultuous process can take generations and can undermine the unity of the culture. Unsurprisingly, the same is true for the church, which is, after all, a cultural reality. The church has a long history of reacting poorly to new ideas, new technologies, and even new instruments. Most of these stories seem quaint now. One need only consider how suspicious church leaders were of musical instrumentation in worship services to realize that our embedded cultural assumptions creep into what we think is good or bad for the community of faith. The assumptions about and fears of the new are often unexamined and without warrant.

That there remains a cultural bias against video games in the church, more than forty years after their widespread appearance to the public, is perhaps unsurprising. The cultural assumptions, especially in more conservative circles, are that they are juvenile, prurient, or just too foreign to the world of useful or spiritual activity. They provide escapist, violent power fantasies that have little to do with the message of Jesus. I disagree with this reaction—that should be no surprise—both because I do not experience video games that way, and because I think the church has a missional responsibility to respond differently than other cultural bodies to new cultural realities. I think this because I believe the church is not merely a cultural body, but the Body of Christ that transcends culture.

In this chapter, I want to consider two possible responses to video games, drawing on previous reactions to popular culture and how popular culture can and should be incorporated into the church's life. On the one side, I will consider the Christian rejection of popular culture as too worldly. I will call this the "Tertullian" approach, after the church father who famously asked, "What does Athens have to do with Jerusalem?" ("Athens" represented Greek philosophy and "Jerusalem" represented Christianity.) The other approach I will call the "Romantic" approach. It is the other side of the coin, the one that sees culture should usually be embraced, though critiqued, by Christianity. The approach is not, of course, limited to the Romantic movement, but the term is wide-ranging here, embracing everything from the Arthurian Romance of the high Middle Ages to the faerie lands of the Romantic Christian authors like George MacDonald, J. R. R. Tolkien, C. S. Lewis, and Madeleine L'Engle. My hope is to show that the Romantic approach is not only the more balanced, considered, and reasonable of the two, but that it also is the stance that is more in line with the mission of the church.

The Tertullian Approach

When we take the Tertullian approach, we believe that the church must always be suspicious of every aspect of culture. We fear the poisoning of the pure and true Christian faith. Lest the true worship of God be tainted by heathen, pagan, or base ideas, the church must hold fast to the tradition that it received from the previous generations. The only surefire way to preserve the church's identity is to keep it holy—set apart from the culture around it.

Such a perspective can look back to the ancient Israelite religion and point to God's commands for the people of Israel to be a distinct and holy people unlike their neighbors who worshipped many gods. It can look to the early church's rejection of the Roman games and the hypersexualized religions of the Mediterranean world. It can point to numerous instances of the church pushing back against its culture and insisting that there is truly only one way to God: Jesus the Risen One. And, as far as this goes, the perspective is correct. But, lest we forget, this perspective is the same that at different times insisted that the scriptures should not be translated into the native languages of the people, the Mass had to be in Latin, and no instrumentation could accompany singing in worship. This is the same perspective that rejected jazz, then rock and roll, then hip-hop. It is the same perspective that rejected the Harry Potter books because they contained magic.

What I find most interesting about this perspective is that, by and large, it is transitory. Its guns are generally aimed at the newest things in the culture, not the parts of culture that have been around for a couple of decades. The same folks who push back against J. K. Rowling don't seem to mind C. S. Lewis, despite there being magic in both authors' works. The folks who eschewed folk music in churches likely thought back to the good old days of jazz. The people accepting classic rock hymns rejected hip-hop, but their kids might push back against the next new thing. Even I wonder about a church that welcomes people with a dubstep remix of "How Great Thou Art." Then again, maybe it would wake some people up in the morning to get ready to praise God.

This rejection of culture by the church is, it seems, the same old thing we see when any person of a previous generation says, "Well, in my day children were well-behaved, women were polite, men were brave, and music was good—not like you have today." Instead of admitting that the attitude is merely a thumbing of the nose at the novel, it is polished with a religious veneer. If something is old to us, then it must be venerable, useful, and necessary to the church. If it is new to us, then we are suspicious. It's not that the Tertullian perspective is without its rationales: Jazz is sex music; look at Elvis's hips; I'm pretty sure Led Zeppelin had something to do with Satan; NWA calls itself a gang; look at how violent video games are; doesn't *Dungeons & Dragons* lead you into a Satanic cult? These assessments are shallow, unengaged, and uninformed. By having such shallow reactions to novel ideas and cultural expressions, the church brings about several bad results.

The first is that it effectively sanctifies a previous generation's culture and demonizes the culture of the rising generations. This has astonishingly bad effects when it comes to the conundrum of evangelizing those rising generations. It makes it clear that church is a place for older people, not younger ones. It also makes it appear as though the church is closed-minded about everything that hasn't been around for at least fifty years.

The second is that it creates a false sense of superiority in the church: we don't do that sort of thing; we know better. Years ago, I had a friend from high school who married the son of my middle school English teacher. By hanging around with my friend and her new husband, I got to know my former teacher and her husband better than I otherwise would have. During that time, Nikos Kazantzakis's novel *The Last Temptation of Christ* came up in conversation. She had heard from her pastor that it was a smutty book and blasphemous against our Lord. I, being a third-year biblical studies undergraduate, felt differently. I had read the author's introduction to the book and had found the book intriguing, though problematic. When I suggested that she might read it for herself and decide, she declined, saying that her pastor's word was good enough for her. From my perspective, there are several problems with this viewpoint. It declines the responsibility to think for ourselves as moral beings by off-loading that thinking onto another human being. The problematic dynamics of power that this sets up are myriad and will be slightly addressed later in the chapter, but it also helps to reinforce this idea of a sanctified set of cultural activities against a base set of cultural activities. We in the church only do the right sorts of things, not like those other people do.

The third problem is that the Tertullian view is somewhat blind to the fact that the church can't escape culture, and that all its practices are inherited from, or modifications of, other cultural practices. The idea that there are genuinely "Christian" cultural realities as opposed to "non-Christian" cultural realities is only true insofar as the "Christian" cultural realities are those elements of culture, past and present, that the church has decided that it will participate in. We must remember that all manner of oppressive activities have fallen under these approved cultural activities, not the least of which was the enslavement and then extermination of Native Americans and the kidnapping and enslavement of millions of African people in American history alone.

The fourth problem of this approach is that it favors older expressions of feeling that may not be accessible to younger generations already in the church. I, for one, find that the words of older hymns, if they are not too stuck on a penal-substitution version of salvation, can be far more edifying than most of what has been written in the last century. The words of "Come Thou Fount of Every Blessing," when they haven't been "updated" are, for me, second only to Schiller's "Ode to Joy" set to the fourth movement of Beethoven's masterful Ninth Symphony when it comes to both reproving and elevating my heart. Indeed, van Dyke's "Hymn of Joy" set to the same piece is almost a peer to Schiller's work. But, barring these masterpieces, I find the musical settings of many older hymns to be too maudlin, at least as they are often played in church. The musical culture of a hundred and fifty years ago has been, in many ways, sanctified in our churches in a way that has left the raucous joy and lament of some of these hymns of beauty inaccessible to us.

Finally, the sanctification of older cultures blinds the church to the valuable contributions of new cultural realities. This isn't limited to their appeal as the instruments of evangelizing the culture that the church is a part of. It also includes the genuine insights into the mystery of God that new forms of culture can offer to the church. God, as infinite mystery, can be approached in infinite ways. That is not to say that all ways of approaching God are edifying, but the good ways of approaching God are endless. The church, by scoffing at novel forms of art, experience, and entertainment is denying itself, usually for at least a generation, new insights into the mystery of the Holy Trinity.

The Romantic Approach

Opposed to the Tertullian approach, I propose that the Romantic approach is a far better solution. From Augustine's incorporation of Roman history, which included a good heaping of legend, to the sometimes more and sometimes less Christianized Welsh myths of King Arthur, to Madeleine L'Engle's science-fantasy *A Wrinkle in Time*, the church has benefitted greatly by welcoming in the culture of the world around it both to enjoy its contribution, and to transform it into something higher and holier than it was. Not only has this process of acceptance of the popular, sometimes pagan, culture into the fold of Christian art and worship given us the mighty works of Bede, Mallory, MacDonald, Lewis, Tolkien, L'Engle, Chesterton, and others, it is a process that has been sanctified by scripture itself. The Bible is replete with myth and legend that were drawn into the warp and weft of Israelite/Jewish and Christian religion.

Two examples will suffice. First, the story of Noah tells of a flood that covers the face of the earth. Many of us who have been to seminary or have studied scripture at the college level and beyond know well that the story is one that has been woven together from at least two different sources, which explains why in some verses six of every clean animal and two of the unclean animals enter the ark, but others mention two of all kinds. It explains why the length of the flood seems to change from forty days to one hundred and fifty days in the middle of the story. It also explains why, though there has been no law given to differentiate clean and unclean animals since that wouldn't happen until the time of Moses, those distinctions are present here.

The two sources are themselves rooted in other ancient Near Eastern stories, such as the Gilgamesh and Atrahasis epics, which significantly predate the biblical account and tell similar tales, but with important differences. In these earlier versions, the gods flood the world because the people they made are too loud. The divine beings regret flooding the world later because they realize that human sacrifices provide them with food without which they would starve. Fortunately, one of the gods had the forethought to tell a man to build a ship and fill it with animals. When the flood was over, the man sacrificed to the gods, they ate the sacrifice, realized their foolishness, and vowed never to flood the world again.

The story is thoroughly pagan. It paints the picture of capricious, selfish, and petty gods. If one were to look at these stories in their original form, one might reject them as too foreign to the Israelite concept of Yahweh, but at least two authors and one editor thought differently. This story of pagan gods destroying the world is transfigured into a picture of the righteous God who hates sin and love goodness. It is a story that shines a light on God that the original stories did not, and by doing so accomplishes both revelation about the character of God and a distinction between the gods who were on offer as alternatives to Yahweh. One of the two authors, as well, carries on the original idea of the sacrificial importance of the animals saved from the flood, and has more sacrificially pure animals saved than those that are "unclean."

Hebrew Scripture is teeming with examples of the adaptation and modification of the myths, legends, and cultures of other peoples. In the New Testament we see plenty of examples of the culture and beliefs of the people of that age entering both the ministry of Jesus and the writings of the Apostles and their pupils. We see Jesus both accepting and modifying the apocalyptic visions of the book of Daniel. We see the author of the book of the Revelation of John doing the same. The book of Jude likely references two nonbiblical books: the Book of Enoch and the Assumption of Moses. Paul relies heavily on

Greek rhetorical style and philosophy. The very idea of "Messiah" was drawn from the prevailing culture of Jesus's day, and doesn't survive in Christianity in any of its original forms. The same is true for the idea of the resurrection that, like the ideas of the heavenly last judgment and the Antichrist, has roots in the Maccabean revolt of the 160s BC.

But, as important as all these examples are, they are drawn largely from religion, especially Jewish religion. I want to highlight a major incorporation by the New Testament that comes from a marriage of Jewish thought and Greek philosophy. It is an aspect of the New Testament that is so deeply ingrained in Christian expression that its roots in Greek philosophy are perhaps shocking. Many have heard of the Greek influence on early Christian thought as an unwelcome addition to the Christian theological tradition. This, from my perspective, is nonsense. Greek thought was always part of the first-century Jewish world. Greek thought permeated a multicultural society forged by the armies of Alexander the Great three and a half centuries before Jesus's ministry. The language, its philosophical assumptions, and its cultural practices, all are present in the first-century Mediterranean world.

Among those cultural influences is a philosophical idea that we will call "The Concept" that goes back to the sixth century before Christ. The philosopher Heraclitus described The Concept as a kind of independent or universal wisdom or rationality. More than three centuries later, The Stoics took up The Concept to talk about the ordering mind of the universe. The Stoics believed that every person shared in The Concept, allowing them to be rational thinkers. In the early first century, while Jesus was just a lad, a Jewish philosopher in the city of Alexandria named Philo took The Concept and applied it to Judaism. He maintained that The Concept was the thing that stood between the perfect God and the imperfect creation—a cosmology that, once more, comes from Plato. He saw The Concept as a kind of intermediate creator. It applied the unchangeable ideas of the Creator to the creation. The Concept is the constant suppliant to God for humanity and distinguishes all things from each other. It is shared by all people. Philo saw this as the principle that dealt with humanity for God who was beyond all comprehension. The Concept, of course, is the Greek term *logos*, which is present in the Gospel of John as "The Word."

> In the beginning was the Word, and the Word was with God, and the Word was God. He was in the beginning with God. All things came into being through him, and without him not one thing came into being. What has come into being in him was life, and the life was the light of all people. The light shines in the darkness, and the darkness did not overcome it.
>
> There was a man sent from God, whose name was John. He came as a witness to testify to the light, so that all might believe through him. He himself was not the light, but he came to testify to the light. The true light, which enlightens everyone, was coming into the world.
>
> He was in the world, and the world came into being through him; yet the world did not know him. He came to what was his own, and his own people did not accept him. But to all who received him, who believed in his name, he gave power to become children of God, who were born, not of blood or of the will of the flesh or of the will of man, but of God.
>
> And the Word became flesh and lived among us, and we have seen his glory, the glory as of a father's only son, full of grace and truth. (John 1:1–15)

Here, then, at the very heart of Christology is the reception of a cultural, philosophical, and novel idea about reality applied to the first-century Christians' ideas about who Jesus

was. Had the early Christians rejected this philosophical innovation blending both Jewish and Greek thought, the church's
Christology would be unimaginably impoverished. But by
embracing this novelty, the early Christians found a category
that allowed them not only to express more fully their experience of the Risen Christ, but also allowed them to expand and
explore that experience in myriad new ways.

The ability of Christianity to take up its culture and employ
it is what keeps it alive and away from stagnation. We must
remember that the Tertullian approach, if taken to its logical
end, refuses the innovations of the Reformation that brought
us worship in our own vernacular languages. It refuses to
accept the drinking-hall tunes that would fashion the settings
for Martin Luther's rousing hymns. The Romantic approach
allows the church to find new joy and insight by allowing it to
express itself in ways that are accessible to its current people.
While, as I mentioned above, van Dyke's "Hymn of Joy" set
to the fourth movement of Beethoven's Ninth Symphony may
remain rousing because Beethoven was a genius of almost
unparalleled might and van Dyke is no slouch, many of the old
hymns do not retain their musical power, even if their poetic
strength remains undiminished. The lyric power of many
hymns becomes more accessible to the worshiping community
when their music is approached from the Romantic position.

The Romantic approach also affords the current population
of the church a dignity that the Tertullian approach does not.
It grants current Christians the honor that is hinted at in Walt
Whitman's poem "Oh me! Oh life!" Whitman wondered what
is the good of the endless years of faithless and foolish life.
The answer comes at the end of the poem:

> That you are here—that life exists and identity,
> That the powerful play goes on, and you may contribute
> a verse.

The catholicity of the church is unboundedly catholic—universal in the ultimate sense of the word. The church is not just for all people, but made up of all people. Its identity is, like Christ, both divine and human. Divinely it transcends its culture, its time, its particularity. The church is present in the first gathering of the disciples of Jesus in the mystery of Pentecost, in a small group of college students who pray together, and in the majestic gathering in Saint Peter's Square in Rome. One church. But many members.

The Romantic approach celebrates the many members. It calls for their gifts. It summons them up, bestows on them the weight of glory, and requires of them their talents, and, yes, their games, their play, and their hobbies are included. The Romantic approach says, "Be the church! Show us the church arrayed as we have not seen it before." Each generation is called up to show itself and to disclose its mysteries of the infinite God. The church may be a "democracy of the dead," as Chesterton said, but it is not a tyranny of the dead. The living have a voice and their voice is revelation to both the generations to come and the triumphant church who has never before seen these wonders among the baptized.

The Romantic Approach Gone Wrong

There are two major ways the Romantic approach can go wrong. The first is that the church absorbs and incorporates the prevailing culture without transformation or critique. The second is that, in the effort to find new things and appeal to the rising generation, it rejects those elements of culture that came before simply because they are not new.

In the first situation, the church looks at the interests, concerns, and identity of its culture and embraces them wholeheartedly. In doing so, it fails to exercise its identity as both a natural and supernatural reality. The church is holy and apostolic. As the Tertullian approach rightly sees, the church's identity as holy and apostolic means it is something other than the culture. Its holiness puts it in the position where it must not accept those elements of culture that can poison it. Its identity as apostolic, usually looked to to justify the episcopate, is also what gives it the power to critique, prune, and incorporate cultural products such as art and science.

I have, in the examples above, considered some lighter and some more serious elements that have come into the church's culture. Perhaps here it is appropriate to show the way that the church has most disastrously applied the Romantic approach. I am thinking of the church's consistent uncritical application of Western culture's understanding of power. Few things have damaged the church more than its wholehearted acceptance of power has. From the priest who is given the cushy position due to his connections, his gender, his age, or his background, to the bishop's mansion, to the papal palace, to the privileged pew for the industrial magnate, to the exclusion of children from spiritual leadership, the church has often uncritically absorbed the world's understanding of who should be in charge, and how and when they should be in charge. The rise of the business-backgrounded bishop in many Western denominations is a good example of how the church has sold its identity to a capitalist culture. I am not overly familiar with the bishops of the Russian Orthodox church, but I would be pleasantly surprised to find out that there was not a similar corruption of the episcopate under Communist power.

It is the world's concept of power absorbed uncritically into the church that perpetuates the protection of those who abuse ecclesiastical positions. It is the coveting of institutional power, the jealous guarding of social influence, and the safeguarding of personal achievement that are at the root of cover-ups of all kinds, which is harmful for all involved. Not only are those who have been wronged incapable of attaining justice, but those who have done wrong are incapable of receiving the cleansing power of truth, accountability, and sacramental reconciliation.

The church's uncritical absorption of cultural constructs of power goes all the way back to the Apostles' assumptions that the structure of the new community would be merit-based. Jesus, echoed by Paul, argues against this. And Jesus should know. It is the uncritical absorption of societal power values that appears in the pseudepigraphal letters of Timothy and lays the groundwork for millennia of oppression.

We can see a second kind of incorrect application of the Romantic approach when the church ignores its traditions, both remote and immediate. The remote traditions of the ancient church—prayers, language, creeds, and rites—can be shuffled aside for "new modes" of understanding and worship. Too often, the church rushes to appease the understanding of the world and leaves behind its distinctive character. The immediate traditions of the church can, as well, be pushed aside for the incoming generation. Does the rising generation not like hymns? Then they can be forgotten and replaced by praise and worship music. Does the rising generation not like that particular food drive, Sunday school, or knitting club that once was so central to the local parish? Then away they go, replaced by whatever new interest is the focus of the rising people who are on fire for God.

The church's identity, both at the macro and micro levels, is defined by its being knitted into Christ by its baptism, which transcends the natural identities of the world and puts them into new relationships. It is true that the philosophical structures of Neoplatonism and the musical tastes of mid-nineteenth century America cannot limit or rule our understanding and worship. However, neither can they be simply jettisoned, for they belong to the church's history, practice, and identity. They are not vestigial burdens but the hereditary lifeblood of the Body.

Some of these breaks with traditions can be merely dunder-headed or inconsiderate, but some can threaten the very identity of the church, the Body of Christ. Take, for example, the valuable concern that male language for God has dominated the church's talk about God and therefore needs to be corrected. This concern is connected to the cultural awakening over the last century and a half to the proper place of women in society as full coequal partners with men (and, more recently, persons of all genders) as the authors and preservers of society. The church's language about the Author and Preserver of all Creation must therefore reflect our perception that one gender does not have a privileged position in being the image of God on earth. A proper Romantic application of this cultural movement would be to begin to include, with concern for the theological accuracy, aesthetic beauty, and historical situation, language that speaks of God in feminine and nongendered terms. It would also preserve the ancient language of the church that goes back to the Gospel of Matthew, especially regarding baptism.

However, an improper application of the Romantic approach would be to jettison male language entirely, to baptize in the name of "The Mother, the Child, and the Spirit" or "The Creator, Redeemer, and Sanctifier." Such formulae, while accurate, are not the historically particular formula of baptism that link us to the whole Body of Christ. The church is more than a body of moral beings following whatever social awakening is currently the hot-button topic. It must remember that the present age gets a vote, but the present age is not a tyrant. We must not let our current cultural situation rule unopposed in the Romantic approach, lest we merely present an equally flawed mirror image of the Tertullian approach.

There are, perhaps, other ways in which the Romantic approach can go wrong. I have outlined what I think are the two most likely and most dangerous. I will move now to out-line a methodology for the Romantic approach that will then be applied to our main topic: video games.

The Christian Romantic Approach in Seven Stages

I now want to propose a general schema for the engagement of the church with cultural concepts. It is a seven-stage pro-cess that I believe will be useful for the church's engagement with all cultural realities. I'm going to first lay out these seven stages and then offer a way in which the church can apply them to video games.

Stage 1: Openness

The first stage of a proper Romantic approach for the church is to be open to new elements of culture, be they artistic, polit-ical, social, economic, or otherwise. Stage 1 should be the consistent stance of the church. It is a stance of listening and welcoming. It is a stance that neither scoffs nor looks askance at new ideas, media, or movements.

Stage 2: Engagement

Engagement means reading books, watching movies, listen-ing to audio programs, tinkering with technology, and having conversations. This stage involves going beyond being open to hearing about things to trying them out. Of course, there are exceptions. If drugs are sweeping an area, the church need not try them out to know if they are bad; we know they are because many people have tried them and the church can be informed by the expert views of professionals who evaluate the ill effects of drug use. There are select elements of culture that are demonstrably opposed to the Christian worldview or measurably destructive. The slippery slope of this position is that a selective refusal of stage 2 can easily become a Tertullian approach: we know that these new kinds of relationships are bad, why engage with them? We know that magic is condemned in the Bible, why read these fantasy stories?

I see stage 2 much like I see the advice that I gave a student who asked about how she should find her own spirituality: try it all. Try every expression of spirituality until you find one that speaks to you. Don't feel bad because the ones you've tried don't speak to you. It was, I hope, understood that there are kinds of spirituality that I was not advocating, like human sacrifice, for example.

I suppose a good rule for stage 2 is that if all the reasonable voices in the church agree that something is bad (heroin, for example), and there is good evidence to back them up, then the church can probably safely avoid it. Otherwise, the church should engage. Again, this is a bit fuzzy, as it is not inconceivable that some voices in the church will regard any novelty as "obviously bad" and thus call for the church not to engage.

Stage 3: Critique

The church's responsibility to critique culture from its perspective as the Body of Christ in the world should not be rejected because it creates tension with the world. The church becomes a valuable friend to the world by offering a critical perspective the world would not otherwise get.

Critique allows the church to say, "We see what is valuable, but here is what is problematic from our viewpoint." It is the stage that, having played card games like *Magic: The Gathering*, and role-play games like *Dungeons & Dragons*, responds by saying, "The lore and fantastical elements are interesting and entertaining, and the play is innocuous. However, the social dynamics of the groups we've played with tend to perpetuate a kind of social ostracizing of the less desirable players." Or, "The play of the game is like any other, in that it entertains, but also creates the opportunity for obsession or extremes of escapism." Such critiques should be leveled equally, uncomfortable as they may be, on accepted pasttimes as well, such as spectator sports. In some instances, the critique may aim at the cultural movement or idea itself. A new social movement proclaiming equality for all may turn out to be a form of oppression if equality is bought at the cost of human dignity, or "all" turns out to be focused on group identity that loses sight of the individual, for example, and the church will have genuinely to reject it.

Stage 4: Transformation

Stage 4 is the stage in which the church, having engaged with and critiqued whatever new cultural element is at hand, has come to understand it to such a degree that it can incorporate it into the church's own life. To do so, the church will have to transform it, which may mean doing what George MacDonald did with fairy tales when he wrote his own Christian stories within the genre. It may mean doing what G. K. Chesterton did with the Father Brown stories, presenting a Christian version of Sherlock Holmes, or what C. S. Lewis did with the science fiction of H. G. Wells in his underread *Space Trilogy*. In other words, it may mean producing Christian versions of the same kind of thing.

The difficulty is, I'm sorry to say, Christians seem quite bad at this most of the time—with the exceptions of the abovementioned masters and a handful of others. We tend, when making "Christian" games, books, and movies, to make cheap, pedantic, and didactic knockoffs. Christian art should be more consistently excellent than average, for the stakes are so much higher.

Another way of transforming a part of culture is to incorporate its forms but imbue them with new meaning. Christmas and Easter stand as perhaps the most obvious examples of this method, but this transformation can also take the form of a participatory framing of activities. By this, I mean that we can take an element of culture, such as playing a game, and transform it from a purely competitive activity to one in which all benefit. The church has done this before many times. Religious life, which takes the regular activities and duties of daily life and reframes them into religious context, is an enduring example.

Stage 5: Contemplation

The stages do not necessarily happen consecutively, where one begins after the clearly marked end of the previous stage. Contemplation is placed second to last because it reflects a deeper understanding of the cultural element that affects the church's life. It requires a process of openness, engagement, critique, and at least an idea of how to transform the cultural elements. This is the moment in the process where the church gleans new insights from the cultural reality. As with all contemplation, there may be a practical or material result from the activity (or practice) of contemplation, and there also may not. Further contemplation of some aspect of culture may open new contexts for contemplating God. This is perhaps the most valuable possible outcome of this process, though the least observably beneficial.

Stage 6: Gift

The gift stage is where the church, having transformed an element of culture, gives the transformed element back to the culture, which has happened many times over throughout Christian history, from the visual arts, to architecture, music, poetry, philosophy, and even war. The idea of Just War comes out of the Romantic approach to culture in which the church debated over whether it was ever permissible to go to war. Just War Theory was the product of Christian openness, engagement, critique, transformation, and gift. The fact that Just War Theory has been misused does not remove the radical nature of its insight, nor should it make us shy away from its gift-nature, but we should instead return to it time and again to judge if it properly applies to a given situation. The main way in which the church enacts stage 6 is by Christians simply enacting the transformed element of culture consistantly.

Stage 7: Repeat

Once the gift has been given back to the culture, the church must retain its stance of openness. It must not think that its work is done, for the work of fallen humanity isn't done corrupting what might be good in culture. The church must be vigilant in its openness, listening, engagement, transformation, and giving.

The Romantic Approach to Video Games

Stage 1: Openness

The church must cease its sneering at video games, cease looking at them askance, and be open to what they have to say. What kind of experiences can people have with video games? What kind of social interactions can be had? These games are the work of human hands, the work of the image of God in the world. They might have something interesting to say. The church should be listening.

Stage 2: Engagement

The church must play video games. This may mean, for those whose responsibility it is to engage with some of the worst of the worst, that we will play games like *RapeLay* and *Hatred*, if only to be able to report back to the larger community that they are genuinely bad so that others may be informed. But, except for the extreme material that delights in the depiction of the harm of people, the rest of the church should be engaging with all video games. This, of course, doesn't mean that priests should be demanding that all their congregants get a gaming computer and fire up the latest first-person shooter game. It does mean that the church at large needs to be engaging with gaming, playing the games, and getting familiar with the culture.

Stage 3: Critique

During its engagement, the church should be critiquing the realities of the world of gaming. The toxic and often anonymous culture that has grown up in online gaming is a good example of an element that the church must reject and hope to excise from gaming, or at least from its own gaming behaviors. Whether the church needs to critique the fictional violence depicted in games like *Call of Duty* or *Doom* remains to be seen. There are voices on both sides of the debate. My own position, which doesn't see the fictional violence as a necessary target of church critique, sees the questionable and potentially predatory practices of ubiquitous microtransactions—incremental payments solicited from players to speed up a player's progress in a game—as far more problematic. I contend that they are created by video game publishers to prey on human psychological tendencies, and are a greater ethical problem than shooting virtual demons, aliens, and enemy combatants.

Stage 4: Transformation

As I have mentioned before, this book is named after a podcast that first debuted in 2011 that I have done with several cohosts, including Father Benjamin Gildas. When he and I started the now-shuttered *Cross and Controller* website, we reached out to video game companies, hoping to get review copies of games. One of the reasons, we thought, even to do a podcast and website on video games and theology was to get free stuff. The first company to send us a box of games was the aptly named Left Behind Games. This box contained the latest version of their *Left Behind* real-time strategy game, as well as a karaoke game with Christian songs that we could never get to work and a couple of kid's Bible games.

That *Left Behind* game is what I think of when I imagine Christians making Christian games. It's a very bad game. Beyond being bad to play, it included the following features:

1. You can play as both the forces of Jesus and the forces of Antichrist. If you play as the forces of Antichrist, you literally can't win the game.

2. If you play as the forces of Jesus, you train your units to become more capable by sending them to a church or church school. If you're on the Antichrist's side, you send them to a university.

3. As a Christian, your job is to convert the enemy. If you can't, you can kill them. You then pray for forgiveness.

This game was theologically reprehensible and beyond bad to play.

Alternatively, a good example of transformation is the video game *Myst* and its sequels. At one point the highest selling video game of all time, *Myst* was made by Robyn and Rand Miller, who are both practicing Christians. The game isn't didactic, has no over-the-top message, and doesn't foist any religious views on anyone, much like *Lord of the Rings*. Instead, it changed video games forever, and thus also falls into stage 6.

Another form of transformation the church can offer to video games is the transformation of the community around gaming. The church can promote fair play, respect, and even the practice of cheering on opponents. The idea inherent in competition that is not transformed by Christianity is that my good is your loss. A transformed concept of play and competition encourages all to do their very best and to root for competitors to do their very best as well. As I mentioned in chapter 1, I have experienced transformed competition with Christian friends on numerous occasions in which we were all trying to shoot one another's characters, and when someone got hit, we congratulated each other and praised the shot.

Stage 5: Contemplation

The church must contemplate what new perspectives on God video games can offer. Are there new ways of seeing old doctrines, new ways of expressing joy, both in God's creation and in creating new worlds and experiences? Can we learn more about what it means to be human by making and interacting with virtual worlds, both alone and in community? Can we experience new kinds of awe while standing in fictional worlds that human beings have made and say, "Lord, You are Mighty for you have created the worlds!"?

Stage 6: Gift

Myst is, as I said, an excellent example of a transformed gift. It is a great example of how Christians can produce a new and interesting interpretation of a cultural experience and give it back. It may shock many readers to know that *Dungeons & Dragons* is, in fact, a good example of the Romantic approach. As Michael Witwer noted in his book *Empire of Imagination: Gary Gygax and the Birth of Dungeons & Dragons*, Gary Gygax, who cocreated the game that was so vilified in the 1980s during the period known as "Satanic Panic," was a practicing, if not always strict, Jehovah's Witness.

The church's gift of transformative gaming can embody the tenets of Christian acceptance, love, generosity, and self-gift. The current tendency of many online gaming communities is either to respond with anger to slights or simply to check out of the community. The church can respond instead with practiced kindness in the face of hatred, and continued participation in gaming communities that embodies the Christian values of loving, not only those who love you, but of those who hate you.

Stage 7: Repeat

Myst was a great addition to gaming. It was a transformative one. We must keep listening, keep engaging, keep transforming, keep giving back, and keep contemplating.

Conclusion

It is my experience that, to greater and lesser degrees, the Romantic approach has already begun in parts of the church. Almost all my gaming friends are Christian. Many of them are ministers. The Romantic approach has begun where it always begins, with the rising generation, and the church should embrace it wholeheartedly. The wisdom of those who have more experience would be very helpful in the church's engagement, critique, transformation, and gift.

Having laid out this process, this chapter concludes the first half of this book, which has been both an argument for and an exercise in stages 1–3. It has also been an explanation of my experience of how stage 4 can happen by describing how my gaming friends have been both gamers and Christians. The rest of this book is an exercise in stage 5: contemplation. The following chapters are an attempt to consider how video games can help us to see our religion and its theology in new lights, which often means drawing on the long tradition of Christianity to work with the new ways of seeing. It is my hope that by engaging in stage 5 I can help to enable stage 6: gift. By helping the church to think about the games they play, I hope this book can help it to think about how to give back to the culture that produced them.

IT'S A SECRET
TO EVERYBODY

THE LIMITS OF KNOWLEDGE

I think the moment the game irrevocably captured me was when I saw the strange house on the cover of Nintendo Power *no. 16. Instead of a video game image, it was a model with people, who had been shaped in putty, leaning out of the windows. Two tentacles, one green and one purple, joined the handful of figures who smiled and waved at each other. From the roof, a telescope extended, and a purple light glowed from a basement window.*

It was 1990, and the game was Maniac Mansion, *created by Ron Gilbert and Gary Winnick for Lucas Arts. The game took place entirely on the grounds of the creepy house that belonged to the Edison family and it asked you to select from a group of kids with different abilities. They had to solve puzzles in the house in order to rescue Sandy, girlfriend of Dave, one of the playable characters. You could play an array of characters, including a punk-chick, a computer nerd, and a music geek. The game promised a sense of endless possibilities and combinations. The house, though much smaller than the worlds of* Zelda, *or* Final Fantasy, *seemed huge and full of hidden secrets.*

71

It was here, with this game, I believe, that my mind opened to the concept of the ineffable, for there is something about Maniac Mansion *that promises a wonder too big for words. It is a wonder that I would find later in the games that partially inspired the Lucas Arts style of adventure, the even more apparently limited text adventures of the world of Zork. These games, so full of possibility, so evocative of the expansive in their smallness, escaped my ability to address them in a comprehensive way. I might know all their secrets, all their puzzles, and even, with Zork, have access to their code. Yet they remain beyond my knowing, beyond my ability to describe what they are and what they mean to me. Though I have beaten them many times, I return, exploring their well-known nooks, delving their dungeons and basements, not merely for nostalgia, but because they remain beautiful, and thus a window into God's beauty for me.*

How Difficult It Is to Know!

One of the most important questions in theology and philosophy concerns how we know things and what we can know. When we are dealing with things on our level of reality, what I called the middle level in the previous chapters, the question is already complicated. Do we know things, or do we just know some perception of them? Are there actually things out there to know, or is reality just our perception of it? And what about groups of things? Do we genuinely perceive something common between the things in those groups, or is the similarity between those things just in our minds? In other words, do all dogs really have some quality or essence in common—what Philosophy 101 classes would call "doggieness," or is the category "dog" just one that we make up to make our interactions with animals easier for ourselves?

Further, is there something different between knowing the laptop in front of me, which I see and feel, and something like multiplication tables? Both are things I know, but I know them quite differently. One I get from experience; the other, though it might have been taught to me through experience, is distinct and apart from any specific experience. This laptop, though it is like others, is unique in the history of the world. Eight times eight will always and everywhere be sixty-four in all places and in all times. This question of different kinds of knowledge gets even more complex when we ask about knowing the laptop, knowing math, and knowing the people we love.

Finally, is there a distinction between knowing why a thing happened and how it happened? Is there a difference between the reason a thing takes place and the mechanism by which it takes place? Many popular scientific writers today would insist that there is no difference, and this seems to be quite true for mindless things. Asking why a tree fell over is essentially the same as asking how the tree fell over. One doesn't usually look for purpose when inanimate objects act, unless, of course, we think that a person has acted on them somewhere along the line. But when it comes to people, it does seem contradictory to say that the "how" and the "why" of an action are the same. Let's consider an example.

Imagine a party of old friends, close once, but now having gone their own ways in life. Among them was one friend, let's call him George, who betrayed the whole group and hasn't been in contact with any of them for years. They have gotten together on this night, perhaps to celebrate a happy event, an anniversary, or to mourn a loss. In any case, they are together, going over old memories, laughing, and remembering things about each other that they had forgotten. Then, though all of them are present, the doorbell rings. Who could it possibly be? Both fear and expectation sweep the room; they open the door and there is George. He steps inside, and, once the shock has passed, someone looks at the old villain and asks, "Why are you here?"

From the perspective of the person who says that there is no difference between why and how, George's answer might very rationally be, "Well, you see, since there is no randomness in the universe at all, and since there is no supernatural interference with the world, I could not help but be here. There is an unbroken chain of events from the Big Bang all the way until now that mean that I must be here. I was born, my body functions as it must, the molecules in my brain are only doing what they must, and, everything following that, I drove here, walked to the door, knocked, and here I am." Such an answer is, of course, unsatisfying. We would rather George say, "I'm here to apologize to everyone," or "I'm here to tell you all what I think of you."

The point of this little excursion into questions of knowledge in our world is to remind us that thinking about what we know about familiar things is complex. That difficulty is increased by an order of magnitude when we start thinking about what we can know about the reality that is above ours. In other words, when we think about thinking about God, we find that we are pursuing a strange and elusive goal.

The difficulties that the church has faced when trying to talk about the central mystery of Christianity, the Incarnation of the Word of God, and the identity of Jesus of Nazareth demonstrate quite well the complexities we are facing when we think about God.

One Letter and One Word

In the fourth century there was a debate in the church that had to do with a single word in Greek. This wasn't a fight over how to interpret a biblical passage, but was, instead, a philosophical argument about the nature of God. A little background is helpful here, since all discussions happen in a context. About fifty years before this fight over one word, there was a fight over a single letter. An Egyptian priest named Arius disagreed with his bishop over whether the divine part of Jesus was really, genuinely, as much God as God the Father was. Arius said that the divine aspect of Jesus couldn't really be God, but must be the first and most exalted creature that God made. Compared with us, that creature was divine, but compared with God, he remained a creature.

Arius's bishop, Alexander, disagreed and said that the divine element of Jesus was as much God as the Father. Alexander and his deacon Athanasius argued against Arius by using the Greek word *homoousios*. Arius opposed this word, which means "of the same being" or "of the same nature." The priest wanted to say that the Father and the Son were *homoiousios*, which means "of a similar nature." In other words, Alexander and Athanasius were saying that the first and second persons of what we call the Trinity were eternally one God and one being. Arius, on the other hand, was saying that they were two separate beings, one of them was God with a capital "G" and the other was a god with a lowercase "g."

A church council was held to solve the problem because significant elements of the church all over the world found they disagreed about this question. They had not realized they disagreed until the two ways of seeing this problem were made clear by the disagreement between Arius and his bishop, and people did what they do: they took sides. So, in the year 325, the Council of Nicaea was convened. It concluded that Arius was wrong and that the Second Person, the Son, was "God from God, Light from Light, True God from True God, Begotten, not Made, of one being (*homoousious*) with the Father." Arius was defeated, his followers vanquished, and Christian orthodoxy won the day.

Except that it really didn't go that way, despite that being the popular narrative many people learn in college and seminary. Instead, after the council things turned, quite quickly, in Arius's favor. Despite being sent into exile, he returned with the permission of the emperor and suddenly most of the

Christian world found itself agreeing with the viewpoint that Arius had put forward. The Son and the Father were not, in fact, one being.

A flurry of smaller councils followed, and for the next fifty years or so, Arius's point of view flourished. But factions grew up quickly. At first, the Arians held to the position that the Father and the Son were *homoiousios*, of a similar nature, but then a group broke off, the *homoian* group, insisting that they couldn't say that the Father and Son were of a similar nature, only that they were similar. After a while, a third group broke off, and these are the folks we are concerned with here. They were called the Anomoeans. They insisted that the Father and the Son were not similar and were not of similar natures, but were, in fact, unalike.

So, a brief review, since there will be a test after this: Arius insists that The Son, the divine in Jesus, has a similar nature to the Father, but is not as much God as the Father. Then, the Homoians break off from his followers, insisting that the Son was only like the Father. Finally, the Anomoeans insist that the Father and the Son were unalike.

The most famous person in this last group—which is to say that he is well known by people who study this sort of thing but remains relatively obscure to most students of theology and history, and is entirely unknown to the rest of the world—is a fellow by the name of Eunomius, who insisted that there was a single word that denoted God: *agenetos*. *Agenetos* doesn't have a direct translation in English, but it means essentially that something doesn't have an origin or beginning. It isn't begotten or created; it doesn't process from somewhere; it doesn't emerge; it doesn't grow out of or emanate from anything. The only thing that is *agenetos* is God. From Eunomius's viewpoint, if the Son of God is begotten, he is not *agenetos*, and, therefore, he is not God. In a simple deductive formulation, his argument looks like this:

1. God is without origin (*agenetos*)
2. If something has an origin (*genetos*), then it cannot be God.
3. The Son of God has an origin (*genetos*) in that he is begotten by God. Therefore:
4. The Son of God is not God.

This one word, *agenetos*, set off a massive chain of theological insights, though often Eunomius is not given much credit. But from the arguments made against him comes a rich and important theological tradition as well as a vision of heaven that is, at least from my perspective, far superior to the one that has traditionally been maintained by the Western Christian tradition.

The God beyond Words

There are, broadly speaking, two main ways to speak about God. The first way is to affirm things about God, which is called the cataphatic method. We do this by saying "God is ultimately good," or "God is all powerful." We think about good things that we know and speak about God as the one to whom they most perfectly apply without any kind of fault or limit. We know there are beautiful things, but God is the most beautiful. We know that the ability to know things is a good thing, and so we understand that God is all-knowing.

We need not limit ourselves to affirming the superlative nature of God's good attributes. By affirming that the good things about our world and us have their origins in God, we are affirming a kind of likeness and continuity between God and God's world. But, from the Christian perspective, God and the world are not the same thing. God makes the world, and the world has rebelled against God, so there must be aspects of the world, such as decay and sorrow, that are not like God. We identify these negative aspects of our world, and then we deny that they apply to God. Thus, we say that God is immortal, though we are mortal. We say that God is impassable, though we are blown about by every passion. We change over time, but God is immutable. This second part of cataphatic theology is usually called the *via negativa*, or the negative way. It is sometimes lumped in with the second method I will talk about below, but to do so makes a categorical mistake. The defining characteristic of the cataphatic way of talking about God is to look at our world and either affirm or deny that God is like those things. We are saying something positively and identifiably true about God when we say that God is immortal. We have an idea—mortality—and that idea comes from our world. We then say that there is an opposite idea, immortality, which we apply to God.

What should be obvious about this method of speaking about God is that all our language about God comes from our world. We, of course, have nowhere else to get our ideas. One might argue that we could get new ideas from God, and to some degree that is valid, but, if we look closely at the Christian idea of revelation, we find that even when God speaks to humans, God uses human language. We can see why that must be: any communication to a person must be received according to the nature of that person. We all know this idea well enough. We often don't speak to children with the same kind of language we use with adults, which assumes a significant amount of life experience and education. We teach children about atoms at a very early age by describing little clusters of balls that stick together with other balls that orbit them. Later, we tell them a little more, and a little more, until, perhaps, they have the math to be able to comprehend what scientists really think about atoms. The same process happens when we learn a new language. We might know only a few words, and so we can receive information in that language only by means of those few words. We would be lost if someone tried to explain something to us with words we don't yet know. All of this points to the fact that communication is always constrained by the abilities of the person receiving the communication.

So when Jesus teaches his disciples about the kingdom of the Father, he teaches them using the world around him. He uses the images of their world to communicate the things beyond them. He cannot tell them directly; they are not capable of receiving an unmediated understanding of God's life. We see Christ casting about to try to communicate something so divine as the realm of God in Luke 13:18 where he speaks the telling words, "What is the kingdom of God like? And to what should I compare it?"

The whole Incarnation of the Word of God is, to a great degree, an example of this phenomenon. It is the infinitely divine God taking on finitude and humanity so that we can speak to each other as people. Of course, God is acting in other ways in the Incarnation as well, but one of the deeply important actions that is often overlooked is summed up by the great second-century apologist Irenaeus of Lyons. He observed that the Incarnation was part of a process by which humanity was being acclimated to divinity and by which divinity was being acclimated to humanity. A great exchange was starting, but it had to begin by the higher descending to the lower to grant it new capacities that it did not have before. This rule is so important when it comes to thinking about God and humanity that the scholastic tradition had a shorthand name for it: the *Quidquid recipitur.*

The cataphatic method of doing theology is ultimately the most natural to us. We view God as one of the things we can think about; we talk about God using the language that comes from our world; and we affirm and deny truths about God. Therefore we speak as if God is one of the objects or people in our world, and, as far as that goes, this is fine.

But there is a second method for thinking about God that has at its heart a deep appreciation for the otherness of God. It affirms deeply the distinction between our world, which God has made, and the God who makes it. It is known as apophatic theology.

Apophatic theology's fundamental observation is that all the categories from cataphatic theology, both positive and negative, do not apply to God because they all come from our world. Apophatic theology rejects the idea that any human thought could genuinely describe that first level of the hierarchy of existence that we have been talking about. All ideas and words live at the second level of reality and they are too small, too weak, and too simple to describe the first level accurately. Thus, one of the great apophatic theologians of the church's history, Gregory Palamas, speaks first of God as the one "who is good," but then quickly corrects himself and says, "who is the source of all goodness." From the apophatic perspective, God is not even to be called "good" because the category is too small for what we would call God's goodness. All good things that we know are finite and only images of whatever it is that God is. We might, in a limited way, say that God is good, but, from the apophatic perspective, we must acknowledge that goodness as we conceive of it, even in a superlative and eminent way, is too small for God's actual divine goodness. We return to George MacDonald's perception that we "cannot think too well of God," which is true from the cataphatic perspective because God is always better than whatever we can imagine. From the apophatic perspective, it is also true because our thoughts about God will never ascend to the mysterious goodness that hides behind the wall of our own limited minds.

This same rule goes for all things about God, including the idea of existence. From the cataphatic perspective, we say God exists. We might even say, with some of the greatest theological minds of the church, that God is "existences itself," but, from the apophatic perspective, we must affirm that God does not exist, at least not in the ways that we can conceive. God is not part of our world the way that we are, and we cannot interact with God in the same way that we interact with the things in our world. From the apophatic perspective, we might say that God is the "source of all being," though God does not exist in the same way that the things that God makes exist.

The apophatic way of thinking springs from the debate with Eunomius. The heroes of the debate, the Cappadocian Fathers, demonstrated that not only can no one word (*agenetos*) encompass and limit God, but, in fact, no amount of words could ever do it. In observing that no words could ever encompass God, the whole tradition of apophatic theology found its fundamental starting point. This discussion of human knowledge, both about things on our own level and the One that is in the level above us, is to point out how confined and limited our knowledge is. Even when we consider the things of our own world, we remain baffled. When we consider the reality above us, we are even more confounded, which leads us to the main point of this chapter, as well as to the point at which video games come in to help us think more clearly about one of the problems involved in thinking about the reality above us.

The Search for Proof

As long as there have been theists, there have been atheists. A person may believe that there is a reality above our own, and a person may equally believe that there is no such reality. Both seem possible to the human mind. And, for every person of faith adjuring a person who does not believe in God to "just have faith," there is a skeptical mind asking, "If God wanted us to believe so badly, why doesn't God just prove God's existence once and for all?" The kinds of things that are often requested are largely equivalent to elaborate parlor tricks with the universe. God might write a message at the molecular level addressed directly to the scientists who find it in a rock that fell from orbit millions of years ago. Such an event would, once and for all, prove that God exists. If "Heya, Michael, this is God, and yes, despite what you've thought, I'm real. Remember that day when you were five and you kicked that ball under that car and then lied about it? I remember it, too, and I forgive you. Love, The Eternal God" appeared under a microscope, how is it that Michael, no matter how skeptical he was, could doubt?

The difficulty with this answer is, even if this were to happen, anyone philosophically predisposed to disbelieving in such events would find a way to discount the evidence. There are many possible links in the chain of getting a meteor from a field to a laboratory to selecting this exact piece of rock to look at and then bringing it to a microscope. In all these links there is the room for doubt. Even the supposedly secret information could be explained away as a story once told to another person and then forgotten. There are plenty of places for doubt to slip in.

The story is not meant to take a stab at atheists. The philosophical predisposition to see or not see what we already believe, a process called confirmation bias, is as typical in theists as it is in atheists. Often, those who have decided that God is always speaking to them will, without any objective indication at all, interpret the most mundane events as deeply portentous. Imagine such a person walking along, thinking very serious thoughts about themselves. From above, a clump of snow falls from a tree branch and plops on their head. The interpretation that "God is telling me to not take myself so seriously" and to have a good laugh at myself might seem obvious—and certainly better than the other possible interpretation, "The devil is mocking me with snow, I must keep on with this serious thinking." We often see what we already think we will see.

My point is not to delve into confirmation bias, but to point out that what an atheist wants in the parlor trick method of divine proof is, ultimately, impossible. Any such trick would have to be both perpetually in front of the person so that past experience couldn't be doubted and resistant to how human knowledge works, so as not to allow doubt about the authenticity of the trick. Having considered the difficulties in thinking about our world and about God, I want to consider how video games help us to shine light on these problems, especially the problem in thinking about God and any demands we might make for proof.

A Solid Box

Let us look at a game. For the sake of familiarity, let's take *Super Mario Bros.* and use it to think through this problem of knowledge. First, we can't use an existing *Super Mario Bros.* game; we will instead have to imagine a future version in which Princess Peach, Mario, Luigi, the Goombas, Koopa Troopas, and all the other characters are self-aware artificial intelligences. When we imagine them, we must not imagine them like HAL from *2001: A Space Odyssey*, nor like the robot GERTY from the movie *Moon*, nor like Data from *Star Trek: The Next Generation*, because they are all artificial intelligences that exist in and interact with our world. Instead, we must think of the self-aware Princess Peach as being entirely unaware of our world because she exists in her own world.

Her experience of existing in her own world will help us to think more clearly about how our knowledge works regarding supernatural realities. Our mental experiment here will take place in four acts: Natural Information, Supernatural Information, Supernatural Interference, and Thinking about the World Above. These four acts will show features of, and difficulties with, the act of thinking about and knowing a world that exists above our own.

Act 1: Natural Information

Before we delve into the question of how Princess Peach might know the world that is above her own (our world), we should think about how she knows her own world. All of this is, of course, theoretical, but not impossible given advanced enough computing power. For her to share a world with other characters, and for her to know them and her world, she must be able to perceive her world. Thus, we will say that she sees her own world, hears it, feels it, and maybe she even smells and tastes it. More likely, she receives information about her world in ways that are only analogous to our senses, since she doesn't have actual eyes, ears, or skin. Perhaps programmers will make it so that the lighting of the game gives information to her through the spots where her eyes are, but perhaps they will allow her to perceive in other ways that don't rely on a lighting model that mimics our reality. The ways in which programmers could allow her to know about her world without having her depend on a lighting model in the game giving her information are far too myriad to consider here. Suffice it to say that Princess Peach knows her world, and she knows the creatures in it. They also know her. Perhaps they communicate with each other using means analogous to spoken language. They need not, of course, since they are computer programs and could communicate in a thousand other ways. But since we made them, perhaps we make them as much like us as we can.

She shares a reality with these creatures, and they have similar capacities. They know the world in similar ways to the way she knows it. They agree that there are blocks over there, a castle back that way, and that Bowser, the villain of the world, is a real jerk.

Act 2: Supernatural Information

Let us imagine Princess Peach is walking along, thinking about her relationship with Mario and how complex it is. Then a voice comes to her and says that she is in a video game, that she is a creature that exists in a simulation, and that there is a whole world outside of her world. The voice tells her all kinds of things about herself and the world she is in and the world beyond her world. Princess Peach has a choice: she can choose to believe the voice or not. There are a lot of possible explanations for what's happening to her other than the extraordinary claim that there is a world outside of her own. Clearly, such a world is unnecessary. Things run along just fine in the mushroom kingdom without some highly unlikely scenario in which it is just a simulation. If she thinks about it, she might ask what is more likely, that a voice from a world beyond decided to take interest in her and tell her that her world is a creation, or that something completely natural is trying to trick her. Maybe it's one of Bowser's evil plots. Maybe the Princess has gone a little off her rocker.

Let's say she chooses to believe the voice and makes an act of the will to accept what the voice is saying. Her world is a creation. With this new information in hand, Princess Peach goes out to tell her friends. She sits Luigi down with Mario and Toad and some other of her longtime associates and lays out the whole situation. They have the same choice, but instead of having the information given directly to them, they recieve it secondhand. This doesn't mean, however, that they have more opportunity for doubt because Princess Peach can doubt her own experience as much as they can. Let us observe some features in this scenario.

First, Princess Peach is given the information by a means that she herself can receive. We imagine that the person in our world, whether a developer or a player, cannot simply yell at the system that is running Princess Peach's world. Or, if they can, it is because that system has a microphone in it and transforms the person's voice into something that can be heard in Princess Peach's world. In other words, a human would have to use a means of communication appropriate to our world and then convert it into a means of communication appropriate to Princess Peach's world. If this isn't the case, then all the yelling at the game system will do nothing because Princess Peach has a nature in which she exists, replete with objects and laws of nature. Princess Peach's world is different from ours, and she can't see and hear the things we can see and hear. She has specific ways she receives information, and, so, if someone is going to communicate with her, it will have to be in a way appropriate to her. If Princess Peach and her friends don't speak, but communicate through other means of information exchange, then whatever the human person is saying or typing must be converted into that medium. If Princess Peach doesn't have the capacity to hear, then the words will never reach her unless they are converted into her means of communication. The rule of the *Quidquid recipitur* applies here just as it does in our own world.

The next thing that we observe is that Princess Peach is not obligated to believe the information that she is receiving. Now if Princess Peach is programmed to believe all things, or to believe all things that come from special locations (like the sky, a burning mushroom, or whatever), then she cannot doubt the information. But if Princess Peach has the capacity to doubt, then she may do that.

So Princess Peach has now received information about her world's existence and, let us assume, she is free to doubt it. That information can come in any way and her freedom remains the same unless she is either designed to not doubt (and thus she is less free) or someone blocks that ability from the world above. So far it seems that Princess Peach's intellectual difficulties look a lot like ours. If someone came to her and said, "What if everything around you isn't real, it's just sensory input but there isn't really anything behind it," she might conclude, like Descartes, that she was real and that she was experiencing things, or she could doubt her whole world, just like we can.

Suppose that Princess Peach sits down with Mario, who, for the sake of our mental experiment, is quite the skeptic. Mario would pose many of the questions above. "How do you know this voice was real? Do you have any evidence of it for other people? If there were such an 'overworld,' why would people from it be at all concerned with the people down here, in this world? Isn't it all more likely that you are being deceived by Bowser, or some other dastardly figure that is far more believable than some world 'up there'?" Princess Peach may not be able to answer these questions.

If this were her entire experience, she would be left with enough to think about for her whole life. However, let's consider a possible next step in Princess Peach's experience with our world.

Act 3: The Supernatural Interference

Up until now, Princess Peach has been told that her world is a world hidden away inside a computer in another, larger world. Let us ignore whether Princess Peach has a concept of a computer or not. She goes back to the place where she heard the voice, curious if she will learn more. To both her great delight and dismay, she does. The voice tells her that not only is her world a creation inside of a larger world, but that this larger world is populated by billions of people who are more completely people than Princess Peach is. Her personhood is modeled on theirs, but it is smaller and less robust than their personhood. She has been made in the image of the people above her, and so has her world. Further, not only are Princess Peach and all her friends small images of the people in the world above, but they are often, if not always, somehow controlled by the people above. Her identity is, in a significant way, composite. She is both natural according to the world she knows, and supernatural. Supernatural here doesn't mean ghosts and spirits, especially since there are such beings natural to Princess Peach's world. Instead, it means that which comes from the world above, which, in this case, is our world. Indeed, this other part of Princess Peach will continue to exist and live when she dies. She is told that there are actions that happen in her world that take place only because the people in the world above make them happen. The world might change direction, or the time of day might change quickly. These are things that the Princess has supposed are natural events with unknown causes. She might even know the natural causes for some of these events.

The question is, what will Princess Peach think of this new information? She might start shuffling through all her thoughts and actions to try to pinpoint which of them was controlled by the outside world. She might look for the "supernatural" elements of her own existence, and very likely, she might not find them. She could think about the events that are supposedly caused by outside powers, but they might look entirely natural to her. She could search for some part of her that can't be explained by the natural world, and will likely fail. Then, of course, she might go to her skeptical partner, Mario, and tell him the information, whose response might be something like the following:

What evidence is there for such a world, Peach? None. It is even more impractical to talk about some kind of supernatural element in you. You are like me, all your actions happen because you want them to, or because that is simply the nature of things. Tell me, do you ever jump when you don't want to? No? Then you are not being controlled. Also, why do you need to explain your existence that way? Isn't it simpler just to say that you are the person who is sitting in front of me? Why should you need some strange, otherworldly person to explain who you are?

All the events of our world are perfectly natural. No one has ever seen a real supernatural event. Everything is explicable by the laws of nature. And anything that isn't, will be one day. If the world rotates at times and we don't see why, surely there is an explanation for it somewhere in the world. Perhaps we may never know it, but that doesn't mean that it's a supernatural event. Isn't it more likely that someone is giving you this information to undermine you, to make your doubt yourself, and therefore to control you?

If such a world existed, let them prove it. Couldn't they write something in the sky? I don't mean the ordered way in which the coins hang in the sky sometimes, that's just a natural phenomenon. I mean, actually prove it. If they are out there, why don't they prove it?

These are damning questions for Princess Peach's potential belief in the world above her. The whole thing, in fact, could look like a villain's plot to confuse and befuddle our hero. She might reject it all as entirely implausible. She has the freedom to believe or not.

Act 4: Thinking about the World Above

Let's consider the possibility that Princess Peach chooses to believe in the world that she has been told about and wants to think about it. If she has been given eyes that see and ears that hear, and that sight and sound have been approximated in her world, then her ability to imagine our world will be greatly increased. Indeed, the more systems in her world that approximate our world, and the more capacities that she has that can receive information from those systems in ways that are like our own capacities of touch, taste, and smell, then the better she will be able to imagine our world.

But it is more likely that she will not have the same kind of capacities. Instead, she will receive information from her world in different ways that approximate the same kinds of information. She may have access to a centralized "manager" object that gives her information about the locations of things in the world and determines whether or not she knows where something is. She will gather the height of an object, not by light bouncing off its surface and into her eyes to be processed by her mind, but by some other means of determining the numerical value of the distance from the ground to the top of the object. She will know that "noise" was made by an object because a numerical value will be adjusted by the "manager" object depending on the original volume of the sound, the direction, and the distance it happened from the Princess. Indeed, she will likely know things in a totally different way than we know things.

If this is the case, then it will be difficult for Peach to imagine our world, and her visualization will be constrained by her experiences. She might be able to say, accurately, once she's been told, that Mount Everest's elevation is 29,029 feet. She has a concept of height; she has a concept of a mountain from her own world, and she can use that knowledge to understand that fact about our world. She has concepts of kingdoms and rulers and people, so she might know that Britain is a nation, that it has a queen, and that the queen's name is Elizabeth II. She knows what it means to find an object in the world and to use that object on herself to increase her health, so she might have some idea about food and medicine, but those ideas will be approximations.

We might also try to imagine what it might be like to force her to believe in our world, which would not be difficult to do. We would just program her not to doubt. Then she would go on believing without question. But forcing her to know about our world would be different, and, perhaps, far more difficult. We could put all sorts of information in her head about our world—pictures, movies, and all kinds of data—but if she is really a person in her own world, then these images could not be anything but "otherworldly" for her. She might experience them as mystical experiences, or she might experience these images as a collection of things that seem either more or less real than her own world. She might, going out every day and seeing the green digital grass, acknowledge that the videos of grass in her head are of the original upon which her own grass is based, but that grass will then appear one of three ways to her. It will either seem "more real" in a way that makes her own grass seem transitory and illusory; "less real" in that it is seen as a "spiritualized" or "idealized" version of the plain, real, simple grass of reality; or, if the graphics have made it such that there is no discernable difference between her world and ours visually, the difference will not be apparent at all. In all these cases, we will have failed to communicate our world to her as the simple, plain, real world that it is.

The classical example of one kind of smaller existence trying to understand a higher existence is the novel *Flatland: A Romance of Many Dimensions* by Edwin A. Abbott, published in 1884. In the novel, a two-dimensional square is introduced to the ideas of a one-dimensional world and a three-dimensional world. It isn't until the main character, A. Square, sees the world of three dimensions that she can comprehend it. This example is well worn, but it is worth noting that the principle has been observed for some time, well before video games were invented. It is hard to imagine a world larger than our own. What is more useful about the video game example is that we are not limited by shapes and emotions as Flatland is, but instead we can conceive of a being with all manner of analogous sense and actions that are smaller than our own.

So What?

What does this mean for us? How does this help us think more clearly about Christian theology? I think this thought experiment gives us two important insights into Christian theology. The first is that when we consider Princess Peach's plight while trying to understand the world above her own, we recognize our own. Just as she might try to understand things like the propagation of sound through the air (which doesn't really happen in video games), we try to understand ideas like how the three persons of the Trinity can be one being. The world above her is a mystery to her, as is the world above us. Indeed, it is even a mystery that the "above" world isn't related to us in terms of spatial relationships at all. The trees in the Princess's world might be near or far from her current position, but they are not nearer or farther from trees and mountains in our world, no matter how far away they are from her. In other words, in her world, two mountains might be two thousand miles from each other, but this does not make one mountain closer to any part of our world than the other mountain. Our world and her world are not related spatially in the same ways.

Further, her knowledge of her own world is limited in a way that is explicable by the fact that many of the things about her world don't exist in her world. They exist in our world. By this, I mean that the rules that govern her world exist in our world and make her world possible. The "what" of her world is available to her. She can go out, pick mushrooms, examine them, and compare their effects. She can do science, but she can't really get at the "why" of her world, since that essentially lies in the world above. Indeed, to really know all the things about her world, she would have to be in our world, since much of her world isn't accessible to her. So it is with our world in which we can know how things work, but the actual nature of the universe, the actual laws of physics, not just descriptions of those laws, are fundamentally beyond us.

In fact, given that Princess Peach lives in a world that we know was created within another world, her intellectual plight looks shockingly like our own. Put the other way around, the state of knowledge in our world looks amazingly like the state of the knowledge in created worlds. We can conceive of a reality above us that we can only think about in terms of our own world, and while the "what" of our world is more or less accessible to us, the "why" of it all is not. This doesn't mean that our world must be created, but it sure looks like a created world. Thus, the first use of this example is apologetic and informative. It explains the Christian view of creation in a way that is accessible to others who do not share it. It reveals the coherence of our position.

The second benefit of this thought experiment is to aid us in understanding our real position with relation to the ultimate mystery that is God. We are simply not equipped to understand God on God's own terms, which is why God doesn't invite us up to God's eternity to learn about God; instead, God became human to teach us in human terms. I had a student once who wanted simple answers to the most difficult and mystical questions of Christianity. I told her that there were no such things; the more we delve into the issues, the greater the questions become. She hated that idea. For her, simple, straightforward answers were the way to navigate the world. I think that's fine if you want a mechanistic world and a mechanistic God, but the reality of Christian faith is that we have a mysterious, wild, three-person God who cannot be constrained by simple answers and who transcends the entire cosmos such that no words, no concepts, and no creation, no matter how big, can ever encompass what it means to be that God. This is genuinely good news because it means that the persons behind our creation aren't just schlubs like us. They aren't simply us writ large wearing transcosmic lab-coats poking at a video game and wondering what will happen next. The Trinity is true mystery, beyond the limits of language. And we are totally dependent on that mystery's grace to receive any understanding at all.

HE EMPTIED HIMSELF

RETHINKING
THE INCARNATION

My quest has been a long one and has taken me to the bottom of the world and to soaring heights. I've delved into the secret rooms of the Flathead Kings, and I've traveled through time. I have collected the great treasures and now, at the end, I stand in the hall of the castle, ready to end the curse that oppresses the land. My options have been limited. Instead of the vast array of human possibilities available to me in my daily life, I have had only a pared down selection of verbs to choose from. I can go, take, get in, leave, drop, and examine. I can open and close, push and pull, and turn things on and off. Indeed, the world that I inhabited, as I played the triumphant text-adventure Zork Zero, *by Infocom Games, was tailor-made for these kinds of actions. The puzzles I engaged have been designed so that I can solve them with this subset of human options. Even though my field of actions has been limited, I have triumphed. I have broken the curse and defeated the Jester. But my victory isn't quite what I was expecting; I am rewarded with a familiar location from the first game in the series,* Zork I: The Great Underground Empire, *during the conclusion. Things come full circle.*

The Difficulty of Thinking about the Incarnation

One of the misconceptions I run into a lot in my introduction to theology classes is that Jesus is somehow partly human and partly divine. Students tend to think in percentages, and the church's language often doesn't help them around this problem. We talk about Jesus being "fully" human and "fully" divine, which sounds like a contradiction. How can a person be 100 percent human and 100 percent divine? This difficulty was, oddly enough, taken as a kind of badge of honor by some of my Lutheran friends in seminary. They insisted that it was illogical for Jesus to be both fully divine and fully human, and they reveled in it. They based their position on some of Martin Luther's views on human reason. Tertullian's voice can be heard here as well, since he insisted the Christian faith "is by all means to be believed, because it is absurd." While I admire a good obstinate belief, I don't think that either the "percentages" approach to the incarnation or pride in the illogical is good. I think there is a fundamental misunderstanding of the Incarnation, especially if we consider it from the perspective of the church Fathers who worked for generations to clarify the issue.

This chapter is an attempt to use the laboratory of virtual worlds to try out our thoughts about the Incarnation. We will proceed by first reviewing the thought process of the early church, which will help us to do two things. First, it will show that the early church was dealing with this Platonic hierarchy of existence when talking about Jesus. We should remember from earlier in the book that this is not some kind of later Greek philosophical addition. The essential structure of this thought can be seen implicitly throughout the New Testament, and explicitly in the Johannine texts. When the church Fathers evaluated the Incarnation in the context of this hierarchy of realities, they did so in a way that was entirely consistent with concepts found in the second chapter of the Epistle to the Philippians. They were expanding and clarifying ideas inherent in the New Testament, but they were doing so with many of the same assumptions about a hierarchy of reality. Once we have looked at how the church Fathers approached the Incarnation, we will turn to the question of how video games as virtual worlds can help us think through some of these problems in a new way.

Truly God, Truly Human

It is no wonder that people asked who and what Jesus was in light of the early Christian belief that he was raised from the dead. Assuming that he was, in fact, resurrected, two significant forces were at work among those who had seen him and those who had been told about his resurrection. The first force was to assign him some level of divinity, which made good sense in a pagan world, and also in a Jewish world that had been infused with Hellenistic philosophy. Again, Philo's Logos stands as a clear example of how these thought worlds overlapped. If the man rose from the dead, especially if there were stories circulating of him working wonders, healing, and exorcising demons, then the fact that people jumped to the conclusion that he was somewhere on the divinity spectrum seems entirely reasonable. We see possible evidence of this rush to divinity in the second letter of John in which those "who do not confess that Jesus Christ has come in the flesh" were considered Antichrists (2 John 1:7).

The second force that pushed against the rush to divinity was the conviction of those who saw Jesus a man. They knew his mother; they knew his brothers. They grounded him in a real place and time, unlike Dionysus, Osirus, or Balder. They were his friends and his family, the people he healed, and the people who had confronted him. They had seen him get tired, weep, sleep, eat, and die. These two forces vie, even today, for a full claim on the person of Jesus. Is he the Jesus of History, or the Christ of Faith? Is he human, or God? Another way of asking this question is to which level of reality does he belong? If he belongs to our level of reality, then he does not belong to the one above us. If he belongs "up there" in the upper reality, then he doesn't belong here.

This push and pull exists in the extremes of Docetism, whose adherents believed that Jesus only appeared to be human, and in the beliefs of the Ebionites and other Adoptionists, who saw the man Jesus as simply a human being whom God adopted. They rejected any sense of divinity as much as the Docetists rejected any sense of his humanity. This pushback against divinity, in the Ebionites, in particular, seems to stem from their Jewish identity and a rejection of the kind of Judaism that Philo represented, which created a kind of spectrum between the Creator and the creation.

This argument about which world Jesus belongs to continued for centuries. In the early fourth century, we come once again to the prototypical Christian heretic. Arius, as I mentioned in the previous chapter, an Egyptian presbyter, challenged his bishop, Alexander, on the matter of how divine Jesus was. Alexander believed that Jesus was, according to his divinity as the Son, eternally God and that there was no difference between God the Father and God the Son except that the Father begat the Son and the Son was begotten of the Father. With that one difference aside, they were equally God: one being, one God, one power.

Arius said that, while God and Jesus were of similar natures, they were not equal.

Both viewpoints found sympathizers throughout the Roman Empire. The First Council of Nicaea was called in 325 and it sided with Alexander, though soon nearly the whole empire was on Arius's side. For almost fifty years, it looked as though the Council of Nicaea and its upstart creed would be forgotten. Through the heroic work of Athanasius, a former deacon of Alexander who became a bishop, the tide was slowly turned. When Athanasius died, his mantle was picked up by the Cappadocian Fathers, who, as I noted in the previous chapter, debated Eunomius. They put the final nail in the coffin of Arius's views and the full divinity of Jesus was established as an incontrovertible doctrine for Christianity in the year 381 at the First Council of Constantinople.

Though the issue of Jesus's divinity was firmly established, there were other problems to be addressed by the church's great minds. There were serious questions about the completeness of Jesus's humanity, as well as important objections about the relationship between the humanity and divinity of Jesus. The most important of these was posed in the late 420s by Nestorius, the patriarch of Constantinople. He accepted that Jesus's humanity was complete; he also accepted that his divinity was complete. He thought, however, that they were related, not as two natures in the same person, but as two persons bound together by the power of the second person of the Trinity, the Son. Nestorius thought that the Son joined himself to the life of Jesus of Nazareth, and that they worked together in perfect harmonious agreement—two complete beings brought together in a kind of perfect marriage.

This idea was opposed by the patriarch of Alexandria, Cyril, and rejected at the Council of Ephesus in 431. Twenty years later, in 451, the Council of Chalcedon reaffirmed its rejection of Nestorius's view, as well as the view of a man named Eutyches, who took the opposite position from Nestorius. Eutyches insisted that before the Incarnation divinity and humanity both existed, but when God became human, the divinity swallowed up the humanity so that there remained only one nature. The church rejected both ideas, insisting that there is only one person involved in the Incarnation, the Son, and that he exists in two natures. That same Son is eternally God and born of the Virgin Mary. That same Son is of the same nature with God, according to his divinity, and of the same nature with us, according to his humanity. According to his divinity, he is immortal; according to his humanity, he died at the hands of the Roman state. This formula, known as the Chalcedonian definition, states that he is to be confessed as one person in two natures. It insists that "he is complete in Godhead and complete in humanity, truly God and truly human." Notice that it does not say "fully" God nor "fully" human. Instead, it says that his divinity and humanity are both complete and true.

I often say to my students that this can be understood to mean, "Whatever it means to be God, Jesus is that, without anything lacking. And whatever it means to be human, Jesus is that, without anything lacking." Even so, the difficulty of thinking about the Incarnation clearly is inherent in the fact that, at its core, the Incarnation is a mystery. It is an act of God, and, therefore, it is beyond human comprehension. We can ask many questions about it, and we can come to varying levels of understanding about it, but its mysterious abundance is so great that it will continue to feed us unendingly with new insights. There are myriad approaches to asking about how it is that Jesus is both God and human. Some of them are more along the lines of the philosophical discussions outlined above. Others can take more cultural, linguistic, or power-dynamic bents. It should be no surprise, given how I have used Plato up to this point in the book, that we will remain, to some degree, in the philosophical realm as we consider how virtual worlds and video games might in fact allow us to think more clearly, or at least more fruitfully, in a new way, about the mystery of the Incarnation.

It is worth pointing out that the hierarchy of realities assumption is completely in keeping with the mindset of Athanasius, the Cappadocian Fathers, and Cyril of Alexandria, who each contended with viewpoints that reduced the humanity or divinity of Christ, or reduced the integrity of the union between those natures in the person of Christ. What we are doing in this chapter is seeing whether a contemporary technological extension of their pattern of thought can be fruitful.

Cyril and the Single "I"

When Cyril of Alexandria challenged Nestorius's understanding of the Incarnation, he essentially asked how many "Is" are there in the Incarnation. For Nestorius, the answer was two. There was the "I" of the man Jesus and the "I" of the second person of the Trinity. This is how many church people think. We want to attribute Jesus's weakness, his doubt, and his sorrow to his "human side" and say that his power and sometimes strange knowledge are due to his "divine side." But this isn't what the church says about Jesus. Instead, it adheres to the viewpoint of Cyril, who argued that there was a single "I" in Jesus—that of the Son of God, the eternal second person of the Trinity. When Jesus says "I," he is pointing at his identity as eternal God. When he weeps at the death of Lazarus, it is eternal God weeping in the flesh. When he doubts, God doubts. When he dies, God dies. All these things are happening because he came in the flesh. Athanasius, a century before, argued that the Word took on Flesh to take on the capacity to die. God, being immortal, could not die. But if God became mortal—a particular person in a particular place and time—God might do what God could not do otherwise. In other words, God can add to God's capacities by becoming something smaller.

The single "I" of Cyril's theology is of paramount importance to understanding the church's view of salvation. God has come near, not to a single person (Jesus) but to all people because God is Jesus. This mystery of God taking on what we might call a negative capacity (the ability to die isn't an "ability," it's the lack of the ability to go on living), is first introduced in Paul's letter to the Philippians:

> Let the same mind be in you that was in Christ Jesus,
> who, though he was in the form of God,
>> did not regard equality with God
>> as something to be exploited,
> but emptied himself,
>> taking the form of a slave,
>> being born in human likeness.
> And being found in human form,
>> he humbled himself
>> and became obedient to the point of death—
>> even death on a cross.
> Therefore God also highly exalted him
>> and gave him the name
>> that is above every name,
> so that at the name of Jesus
>> every knee should bend,
>> in heaven and on earth and under the earth,
> and every tongue should confess
>> that Jesus Christ is Lord,
>> to the glory of God the Father.
>
> (Phil. 2:5–11)

Paul wrote his letter within twenty-five years of Jesus's crucifixion. It is, therefore one of the earliest statements about Jesus that we have from his followers. As New Testament scholar and theologian N. T. Wright has pointed out, the only clear and sufficient explanation for this viewpoint is that the murdered man, Jesus, was raised from the dead.

All of this is to say that the model that we are about to consider regarding video games has a long-standing tradition dating back to the earliest Christian expressions, refined and formalized in open intellectual debate by great minds of the early church, and confirmed as part of our sacred tradition through the works of ecumenical councils. It has been affirmed by saints and scholars for centuries since. It is not, of course, the only way to approach the problem, but it is *a* way with ancient roots. With that in mind, we turn to the world of games.

Emptying Oneself

Let's go all the way back to that moment that I was standing in the hobby store judging the guy who was telling me about going down into Hades and getting his grubby mitts on Thor's hammer. My thought at the time was, "You didn't do that, it's just a game. You just imagined that you did it." But time and contemplation have changed my mind. I want to consider the fact that games like *Dungeons & Dragons* allow us to create a lived analogy of the Incarnation. And video games provide an even more robust analogy that works with the same Platonic idea that there are levels of reality. When we think about the Incarnation, we tend to think about two levels of reality: the Divine and Creation. In the gracious act of Incarnation, the Divine identifies with creation and chooses to live as a human being: to be born; to have a language, a culture, a heredity, a family, a worldview, friends; and, to die. All these acts are not natural to the first level of being. God must descend to our level of existence to be able to do these things. God does not have a gender; Jesus did. God does not have an age, but Jesus did. Indeed, all the qualities that the second person of the Trinity takes on by being human are limitations that God does not naturally have; they are also particularities and capacities natural to being human.

God both empties Godself by being human and retains God's own eternal divinity. Heaven isn't empty while Jesus is giving his friends nicknames and healing the sick. Jesus is male in his humanity, but the Second Person is not bound by human gender. The Second Person of the Trinity adds a reality to Himself as opposed to merely exchanging natures.

When we enter a world like that of *Super Mario Bros.*, the *Uncharted* games, or *Star Wars: X-Wing* we do a similar thing. By acting in those worlds, we become an agent, a specific member of those realities, and we both gain new capacities, and we limit ourselves. I can do all kinds of things in real life that I can't do in *Super Mario Bros.* For example, I wrote this book in the real world, but I can't do that in most games. In the gaming realm we naturally say, "I did it," "I defeated the boss," "I shot down the TIE Fighters," and "I found the lost city," because we understand that we are the actor in these situations, though they are virtual. We inhabit those worlds. We do so through the tools, or as Athanasius might say, "the instrument" of the virtual bodies or representations in those worlds.

The Limitations of the Analogy

There are, of course, significant limitations to this analogy. The two that are perhaps most important are the moral limitation and the limitation of being, or what we might call the ontological limitation.

The moral limitation is that this is not what Paul meant when he said that we should have the same mind that Christ had. He was not advocating that we should descend from one reality to the next and find ourselves linked to lower natures, at least in the way that we are talking about here. Paul's point was that we should not think ourselves too good to descend to those who are "lower" than we are, especially in the eyes of our prejudices and culture. Christ did not think that equality with God to be something to be held onto in the face of the need of others. We cannot hold onto equality with this or that social class, this or that clique, this or that group that is "better" than another when there is need. We must be willing to let go of our supposed superiority and serve each other, laying ourselves down for the good of each other. This descent is present in our social, economic, and intellectual lives, but we may also see here the roots of another kind of descent being advocated. The nature that Christ comes to is so far below God that a comparison is difficult to imagine. We might find ourselves, therefore, compelled to consider which natures in our own world we consider "below" us that we should turn to in service, not superiority. The roots of a strong theology of environmental stewardship are here. We must not confuse the philosophical structures that we are using to try to think more clearly about the Incarnation with the main point of Paul's admonishment. His primary point isn't the relationship of levels of reality, but service. He is using the illustration of these levels of reality to make an ethical point.

The second limitation of the analogy is the limitation of being, or ontology, the study of being and existence. There is a very complex argument to be made about how Christ's descent into our world is different from our participation in video games. It has to do with how our world relates to God's existence when compared with how video games relate to our existence. The brief version of this argument is that the creation, while dependent on God, exists apart from God, and that video games do not exist apart from our reality, though they do exhibit a set of characteristics that are a specialized subset of the characteristics of our world. In other words, God and creation are not the same thing. But video games are part of creation, part of their "parent" reality, and thus our move into them is not the same as the Second Person of the Trinity's move into our world.

While this argument is an interesting one, it is not the primary problem with the analogy when it comes to ontology. That problem is, instead, about permanence. When I play a game, I pass in and out of it. I play Zork for an hour or two and then I put it down. For the time I played, I was both in my world and in the Great Underground Empire, but when I stop, I also stop being the adventurer trying to collect treasures. I no longer am in danger of being eaten by a Grue. I lose nothing of my identity or existence. Instead, I have gently added a new way of being and acting to myself for a moment or two and then have just as gently removed it.

This is not the case for the Word of God. The Second Person of the Trinity irrevocably takes on humanity and is Jesus, son of Mary. The divine doesn't lightly take up humanity and lightly lay it down. Jesus is the Word of God and is so permanently. We are not capable of this kind of permanent adoption of lower natures. We can take on these lower natures for many reasons, but we put them down when we are done. The Word does not take on human flesh and then put it down.

There may be a counterargument to this objection that has to do with the fact that human beings are not, as we often think, just the latest versions of themselves. We are historical persons from birth until we die. To be me is not to be my most recent experience of myself, but instead to be the whole of my lived personhood. If this is the case, then by interacting with virtual worlds, I do irrevocably add them to my existence. I choose, at some point, to make them a part of my historical identity. The same can be said, and perhaps more importantly, of the ethical issues above. We add identities to ourselves by our actions. We know that Christ thinks it is important that we add the identities of those in need to our own identities by giving ourselves away to them. Whether or not virtual identities will have any import or impact on our identities in the long run is entirely unclear.

Freedom and Control

There is another insight video games can give us regarding the Incarnation. In the thought experiment in the previous chapter, one very glaring question might have jumped out: how could it be that Princess Peach, being an artificial intelligence, is controlled by a person in the world above her. Aren't those two ideas entirely contradictory? The answer is they are not—if the people who programmed the artificial intelligence allowed for it. Admittedly, we are positing a lot of hypotheticals here, but I'd like to take a moment to consider what such a computer program would look like so that we can use that idea to think about our own existence more clearly. One can design at least two kinds of computer programs. The first is a closed program, and the second is an open one. The closed program functions without any external input to help it make its decisions. The open program allows for information to come in from outside—a user or another program—and responds to that information.

Closed Computer Programs

There are, by and large, relatively few closed programs. Often a program will be closed in its early stages so that it can be tested, but usually that is only in preparation for opening the program up to outside input. A closed program will, if it is truly closed, run precisely the same way every time. In a truly closed program, there can be no chance, no randomness, and no variation because, in computer programs, chance and randomness are created by referencing things outside of the program itself. This might be user input, or it might be a table of numbers that the program looks at to create the illusion of randomness, or it might even be the current date and time, which, unless it's hardcoded into the program, isn't available to a closed program.

It's easy to see why there are so few closed programs. A program that simply did the same thing every time, that couldn't look for information from the computer it's running on, or couldn't look at files, or the internet, or take input from a user, isn't very useful. It is worth saying that the closed program model of the universe is, ultimately, what we must have if there is no supernatural reality outside of our universe. No matter how we cut it, except by referring to mysterious "randomness" (a term that just means that we don't know the cause of an event), a closed universe is a mechanistic one. Not even quantum mechanics can get us out of this closed system, unless the quantum realm is ultimately open to supernatural direction.

Open Computer Programs

All video games, by definition, are open computer programs. They take in information from the user to direct how they will act. Because computers are complicated, there are also two kinds of open computer programs. The first takes in information that doesn't change its operations. The second, which I will discuss below, and which I call "responsive computer programs," changes what it will do based on the inputs. In the first, the processes run by the program are substantially unaffected by the outside input. Take, for example, a program that converts one kind of audio file into another kind of audio file. It doesn't matter what's in the audio file, the process will be the same. The program goes out, looks for the audio file, and does its work. It gets information from outside of itself, and goes about doing what it does. We might think of the analogy of a rock sitting on a cliff. Gravity is pulling that rock and the ground beneath it together. If I come along and kick the rock, I have added force and might send it flying off the side of the cliff. In that case, the operations of nature don't change in the slightest. Gravity keeps pulling and the rock falls.

Extending this analogy, we might ask whether such a program might not simply function within its own general world (the computer), but also take inputs from things totally outside of its world, such as a person sitting at a desk. You might have a simple program that tells you the first letter of any word you type in. It doesn't matter what the word is; if you type the word in, it will tell you what the first letter was. The program doesn't supply the word, nor does it go out and get the word. You put it in—someone who is totally outside of the program. You're not interfering with how the program works; you're fulfilling the program's purpose to be interfered with from outside. From the Christian perspective, most of the universe can be described similarly. It can receive information from the outside, and when it does, it keeps chugging along, integrating that information into its normal processes. Let's go back to the rock on the cliff. If we think about it, it doesn't matter if the thing that adds the force to the rock is natural or supernatural. If God should redirect already existing energy in the air to push the rock off the cliff, everything still goes on as it would if the thing that knocked it off was a foot or another rock. The universe doesn't do anything differently when supernatural causes are introduced, it just does what it would if the cause were natural.

The ability for creation to accept these kinds of external supernatural inputs is called "obediential potency" in theological circles: a potential in creation to obey its creator. If such a potential exists in creation—and Christianity has largely maintained that it does—then the universe is like this first type of open computer program. It has its own integrity, it does its work as it normally would, and it can receive information from the outside of its system and incorporate that information.

It is worth noting that the principle that I mentioned in the previous chapter, the *Quidquid recipitur,* also pertains to this situation. If information is fed into a video game, it must come to it in a form that it can receive. We have all probably had the experience of trying to play a video or an audio file on our computer that produces a message like "unrecognized video codec" or "unrecognized audio format." This, on a technological level, is the *Quidquid recipitur* in action. You cannot make a video player play Microsoft Excel files, nor can you make your favorite music player play photos. The information coming into the program must be information that it can naturally consume.

Computer games are the same. When I play a game and it needs to produce a random event, it will often create a random number object in its code. This is not real randomness, but instead it is something that looks up information from tables of numbers that create the illusion of randomness. Those tables of seemingly random numbers do not exist in the game; they exist somewhere else on the computer that's running the game. To use those numbers, the game must reach out, grab information from those tables, import it into a form that the game can consume, and then act accordingly. There is a process, then, of taking information that doesn't belong to the program and translating it into a utilizable part of the game's execution.

When we apply this analogy to the universe, we can see that any supernatural event is just a natural event that has gotten its causes from eternal inputs. There can be no supernatural events in our universe that aren't also natural events because of the *Quidquid recipitur.* An event in the universe must be natural because that's what it means for an event to be in our universe, but the cause of the event may come from the outside. Take, for example, the possibility of Jesus walking on water. I had a professor of astronomy in my undergraduate program who believed that Jesus had walked on water, but that it just so happened that when he was doing that, all the water molecules were pushing upward so that they could support his weight. He believed, if I remember correctly, that the mechanisms of the universe had been devised so that at the precise moments of Jesus's jaunt upon the sea, those precise molecules would be doing a thing that molecules naturally do, though rarely in such coordinated patterns.

While I think that is a logically cohesive account of the walking on the water, I do think there is a problem with his take on nature because it proposes that our universe is like a closed computer program. There can be no outside influence. But, as we have seen, closed computer programs always run the same way. If this is the case for the universe, then God designed the universe precisely as it is with disease, despair, and death camps. This flies in the face of the Christian belief and the biblical witness that God created the universe good and did not create moral evil.

It seems equally logical to say that God knows how the universe works intimately—God made it, after all—and the ability to create causality at any given moment is as easy as creating the whole of the universe. If this is the case, then the universe can accept the input that says, "Cause this molecule to be pushing up at this time." This either translates into an immediate change in the molecule itself or it finds some lower down reality or a reality farther back in time to create the response. God need not even introduce new force, but may simply redirect force that already exists, in an analogous way to how I can direct a spaceship moving on my screen with the push of a button because the computer code allows me to do so.

Responsive Computer Programs

The second kind of open computer program, the responsive open program, is one that changes what it does based on input. These programs are the ones we interact with most often. The copy of Microsoft Word that I'm using is such a program. As I type words, it seems like the first kind of program, the one that will do the same thing no matter what I type. However, I can also select text, change the font, add footnotes, do a spell check, and so on. I tell the program what to do next, and it does it, I hope. Most video games are responsive open programs. They take in input from all sorts of places: the internet, a controller, a keyboard and mouse, files on the computer, a game console, or a phone, and all manner of other sources. There have been games that have taken input from how much sunlight is around. We not only control the information that the game processes but also influence which processes kick in and start churning.

What does this have to do with freedom and control? How does this help us to think about Princess Peach as both a conscious being in a game world and a persona that someone can take on as a player? How does it help us to think about the Incarnation? Much of this has to do with how we conceive of human freedom. To consider this, let us think of the human person as having three layers to their free will. The bottom layer is a collection of possible objects of desire. These can range from personal glory to moral perfection to having sex with this exact person at this exact time to eating the rest of the pie to helping the homeless man on the corner. The vast array of possible objects of desire forms the natural scope of human free will. This doesn't mean that it encompasses everything we might desire, since we might desire things that don't fall within its scope. We might, for example, desire not to have free will, or to be a pterodactyl. Neither of these options is open to us as human beings. We are free to want them, but we are not free to will them in the sense that we orient ourselves toward actualizing them.

The second level of our free will is made up of those things that are immediately present to us as possible objects of the exercise of our will. As I write this, I am in a coffee shop, my glass of iced tea is almost empty, and a new barista has just walked by. It is a cool but sunny day outside. The range of my possible actions, the objects toward which I can exercise my will, are incredibly particular to my context. Of course, with the advent of the internet, that array of options is far greater than it once was. Forty years ago, sitting in a café, if I wanted to tell my mother than I loved her, I would have had to go in search of a phone and to give her a call. If she were not near a phone, the exercise of my will would be frustrated. With my cell phone, I can text her at any time.

The third area of free will is the thing that I am willing at any given time. I might desire to refill my tea, but instead I'm plugging away at this chapter. I'm acting on my will. I have directed myself toward this action as opposed to many of the other actions I could be taking right now.

The three levels of freedom, then, are the scope of human freedom, the immediate scope of my own freedom, and the exercise of my freedom. Our culture has largely taught us that we are in complete control of our freedom, but that is not the case. There are many factors that condition that second layer in ways that, for all practical purposes, limit the absolute options to far fewer practical operations of our will. There are actions that I could take at the moment that have not even occurred to me. There are multiple filters between the third level and the second level that control which objects are available for me to orient my will toward. There is my practical situation that presents multiple possible objects of my will. That second level of freedom, which is where my free will can operate at any given time, is also limited by my conceptual framework that is created by my culture, including my language, and my own personal habits. If I am a person who has habitually taken to saying rude words to strangers, then the possibility of speaking rudely to the new barista is presented to my will as a possible action. If, instead, I have habitually made a habit never to speak rudely to strangers, the idea might pop into my head as I'm trying to think of things that aren't really part of my world on a daily basis, but being rude to a stranger for no reason doesn't really form part of this second layer of my freedom.

Therefore, we have some control over what options end up in the second layer of our freedom, but we don't get freely to pick what ends up there. Our freedom mainly exists in the choosing of one of the things from the second layer to move it into the first layer, from possibility to actuality.

This description, which is complex, is still a vast oversimplification, as it doesn't address the strength of our will, the strength of the desire to act certain ways instead of others in that second layer, and other factors. But what I want to point out here is that the way in which Princess Peach might be a free-willed character, as well as one that can also be controlled by a player, is by the player having control over the filters from stage one to stage two. By controlling what comes from her natural freedom (first level) into her practical realm of freedom (second level), the player can allow her to choose while also controlling her. Since human freedom doesn't largely exist in the first level of the will, but instead in the exercise of choosing from the second, there is no impingement on the character's freedom. If we add in the ability to increase desire for one object in the second level of the will, and decrease the desires for other second level objects, then we further exert a level of control that brings about her free choices in line with our own desires.

Beyond being an interesting intellectual exercise, this also gives us insight into the freedom of Christ as a being who is both perfectly human and perfectly divine. If the freedom of Christ is perfectly human, and he exercises his human will perfectly, then this video game example can give us a good analogy for how the divine could work with the human will of Christ. If Christ's humanity was unfallen, which is a doctrine of the church, then the scope of his freedom existed purely from his unfallen human nature. His first stage of freedom was populated only by those things that are naturally human and thus naturally good. His second stage of freedom possessed only those options that came through from stage one. Both his culture and his own undamaged psychology and history were the filters. Thus, his perfect freedom existed with a realm of perfect will. The supernatural element added to his freedom existed by expanding stage one to include not only those things that are possible to a human, but also those possible to God. Thus, he can love humanity, not just as a perfect human, but also as God loves humanity, which not an option open to us unless we, too, are united to divinity.

The union of the divine will with human will in Jesus can be conceived as functioning in this way, completely within the bounds of human nature and expanded and strengthened by his divinity. Fallen human beings, however their fallenness is communicated, have unloving actions included in our level-two freedom. Christ's divinity protects him from this defect. Christ's free will therefore functions freely in union with his divine will. Indeed, the divine can feed specifically from the level three will into the level two will as it chooses without any violence to human nature. This is even more the case if we acknowledge that God is often the author of this specific "surfacing" of possible actions from level three to level two. And, if the witness of millions of churchgoers who feel drawn to perform an act they hadn't otherwise been thinking of doing is any indication, especially if they feel it strongly out of the blue, then we must admit that God does interact with the human will in this way while preserving its freedom.

There is much more we can say about the question of freedom as it relates to models of computer programs as analogies. We might even ask questions of how a computer program might choose something other than what we wanted, despite our filtering of options. We might then delve into the realm of a hierarchy of possible goods, or we might tackle the tough nut of evil, but these are areas of further exploration, and our discussion has gone far enough for a book of this scope.

THE MASS EFFECTED

CAN THERE BE VIRTUAL SACRAMENTS?

I'm walking in the rusting hulk of an old aircraft carrier. The dilapidated behemoth is grounded in the Capital Wasteland, the remains of Washington, DC. The hallways are dingy, but the place is not abandoned. It has become a haven for a group of people who are trying to eke out some kind of life in a hostile world. This old machine of war, long past its ability to serve its original design, has become a haven known as Rivet City.

It's Sunday morning, and I'm walking toward St. Monica's church. I can hear Father Clifford telling the story of St. Monica whose son became a wicked man. I hear him regaling his small congregation with the tale of how she prayed for her son, how she forgave him for his cruelties, and how God preserved her through all her troubles. When the sermon ends, the priest calls for the congregation to pray to God and St. Monica. It is a Catholic church and, thus, I expect there to be the loaf and the cup, but those elements are absent. It's as if these Catholics have forgotten what it means to be Catholic. I leave, feeling unfed.

Years later and farther up the coast in a town called Diamond City, I enter a small, one-story building to find a couple of benches set up in front of a *podium. Two citizens of Diamond City sit quietly while a man named Pastor Clements stands by. I speak to the pastor, noticing his collar, and wonder what denomination he might be. His responses, however, indicate that he doesn't hold to any one God, but instead to the idea that there is a God who provides a quiet place for people to contemplate. I sit and contemplate, but I wonder how I'm supposed to contemplate the Almighty, as Pastor Clements suggests, if I don't have any structure to my thought. I leave, feeling unfed.*

I, like many others, wander the wastelands of the Fallout game series, wondering how it is that in times of radical need, religion hasn't grown to meet that need. Despite vast historical precedent, the authors at Bethesda Games decided that after a war, most Christians would just give up their faith, Jewish people would abandon their synagogues, and the mosques would be empty. In the stretches of rubble and ruin, the Body and Blood of Christ are not to be had and no confession can be made. The waters of baptism, at least the ones that the Spirit moves upon, are still.

Virtual Worship

When I was visiting universities to see where I might go for my PhD, I took a trip to nearby Princeton Theological Seminary. While visiting with different professors, I was introduced to a student who built the first church in *Second Life*, a virtual world populated by thousands of players. The idea intrigued me. Could people worship God in a virtual space? If they could, what were the limits?

A couple of years later I was back at Princeton, only this time for a meeting of the Mercersburg Society, a group of sacramentally and liturgically minded Protestants, largely from the Reformed tradition. Theresa Berger, a scholar from Yale, and I had a conversation about the idea of virtual communion. We both were concerned with the question about whether a person could receive a sacrament in a virtual way. She was, at the time, in favor of the idea, and her 2017 paper, "Participatio Actuosa in Cyberspace? Vatican II's Liturgical Vision in a Digital

World," is a more developed exploration of the idea. In both our conversation and her paper, she mentions a blog post by Paul Fiddes, a British Baptist theologian. The post, which has since been taken down, suggested that communion is possible for avatars, and that they would receive grace according to their nature when they did so. This chapter is a response to that idea, and the world of ideas that goes along with it. I have never been virtually baptized, received the Eucharist, or been ordained as a priest. And, while some of these actions have been approximated or fictitiously affirmed in the games I've played, none of them, I will contend, are possible, even analogously.

Worship in Our World

This book isn't long enough to describe the all the various ways we can talk about what happens when we worship, but it perhaps suffices to say that our worship is a complex interplay of the internal, external, natural, and supernatural. Internally, we have the intricate, tired, excited, angry, sad, and bored experiences and thoughts of our personal worlds. When we worship, we are oriented toward an action and its end. We ask, we give thanks, we praise, we may even accuse or curse. All of these actions have a specific interaction with our Creator, Redeemer, and Sanctifier.

Externally, we say words, sing songs, ask for mercy, pray for justice, listen to the proclaimed words, and offer peace to those around us. Our internal experience, of course, doesn't have to match our external one. We may be thinking of vengeance as we offer Christ's peace to one another. We might be asking to be taught a melodious sonnet sung by flaming tongues above while wanting only to know what the score of the game was or whether our boss has e-mailed us back. We might hear peace but feel convicted. We might be told good news but feel like that news is anything but.

On the natural level, all these things are happening in the biochemical complex that is our body in an incomprehensibly complex natural relationship with the wood of the pews, the light coming through the colored glass, and the other biochemical masses around us. We sense the world around us, we think our thoughts toward God and neighbor, and we enact our worship, whether it is a knelt prayer by the bed, an early Mass on Sunday, or an evening worship service with our college friends.

Beyond the natural is the supernatural element. Our orientation toward God and neighbor, or, in our brokenness, toward our own selfishness, is engaged by God at a level that is not restricted to the laws of psychology, sociology, biochemistry, or Newtonian or Quantum physics. The supernatural meets us in these moments in ways that are beyond our ability adequately to describe, and for good reason. The world in which our descriptive powers work is precisely the world in which we live. Our language points to the things that we can experience and imagine. God's existence is beyond that, and thus God's response to us is primarily in the world beyond words. In other words, God's participation in our worship, whether it is a divine approval and elevation or a divine condemnation of our hypocrisy, is mysterious. God's activity in worship is, in many important ways, the preamble for our actions. We can pray all we like, but if the Spirit is not present to fill us—whether we feel it or not—and the Son is not in our midst, to bring our prayers, praises, and supplications to the Father, then we do not perform Christian worship. For the worship of the church is primarily the church's participation in the life of the Trinity, into which the church is invited through the Incarnation of Jesus. All the above mentioned biochemical, social, and psychological elements are secondary and are, to a great degree, the fumbling mimicry by imperfect and often rather shoddy people of that elegant, eternally perfect self-gift of the Triune life of God. We can participate in the life of the primary participants (the three persons of the Trinity) as secondary participants because Christ has come to us and pitched his tent with us. The worship of the church is both divine and human because Christ is divine and human. *We* participate because he is one of us. We participate with *God* because he is God.

This gift of worship has several special and sacred signs that we call the "sacraments." In the Episcopal church, we have two sacraments and five sacramental rites. As far as I can tell, this is nothing more than a word game used to appease the historical Reformed and Catholic traditions. I see no difference, though I would be happy to be corrected, between a sacramental rite (a rite that enacts a sacrament) and a sacrament itself (which is enacted as a rite). These seven sacraments are those specific actions that are described as primarily the acts of God among the people, and secondarily the acts of the people. These seven acts of God—Baptism, Holy Eucharist, Reconciliation of a Penitent, the Order of Marriage, Ordination, Confirmation, and Ministrations to the sick and dying—are the places where we insist that God is the primary agent and we are vehicles and recipients of this divine action. These actions are forms of communication. They aren't always communication of intellectual information. We don't learn new facts when we eat the bread and drink the wine. They are self-communications from God to us. In other words, they are acts of revelation, for God, as George MacDonald points out, is a God who is always revealing God's self in all of God's actions toward us. In an act of revelation or communication, for the communication of God is always revelatory, there are seven aspects to consider. I will outline them below and talk about each.

1. The Revealer

   The first element to consider in an act of revelation, whether it is a revelation that the cable bill hasn't been paid, that your spouse hasn't, in fact, forgotten your birthday, or that God is a righteous and merciful God, is the one who is doing the revealing. In the three examples given here, the revealers are the cable company, your spouse, and God. Of course, the first two could be other people. Your roommate might tell you that the cable wasn't paid, or your best friend might end your heartfelt pity party by telling you that, despite appearances, your spouse has something great planned for your birthday. But to keep things simple, we will assume it's the cable company and your spouse.

2. The Thing Revealed

This is the information that is to be communicated. It is "the cable bill wasn't paid," or "your spouse remembered your birthday," or "God is merciful."

3. The Mode of Revelation

The mode of revelation is the way in which the revealers choose to communicate their information. For the cable company, it could be a bill, a phone call, or the shutting off of your service. Your spouse might choose to let you know through a gift and card left on the dining room table, a big surprise party, or a simple "Happy Birthday." God might draw your attention to a story of Christ's limitless mercy in the Gospels.

4. The Media of Revelation

The media of revelation are those vehicles that carry the mode of revelation to us. These are the messengers. The bill, as the mode of revelation, comes to us by means of light reflecting from the paper or coming from the computer screen. The sound of "Surprise!" as you walk into the dark room, or the feel of the gift under your fingers in the dark dining room before the sun comes up, both are media of communicating the act of surprise and the presence of the gift. Your reading of the story of Jesus and the woman caught in adultery would deliver the story God has drawn your attention to in a different medium than if you heard the story preached at church.

5. The Receiver

The receiver is, of course, the person getting the revelation. It's you when you turn on the television to find that the cable is out. It's you when you wake up and find your spouse there with a card singing out of tune. You are the one receiving when you read that Jesus will not condemn the woman. You get the revelation.

6. The Capacity for Reception

The capacity for reception is that ability that you have, as the receiver, to receive the revelation according to the media by which the revelation, in this mode, is delivered. This means that if the bill from the cable company is written in ancient Greek, and you don't read ancient Greek, you don't have the capacity to receive the message. If your spouse flashes a huge "Happy Birthday" sign in your room in infrared light and you don't happen to have your infrared goggles on, you won't see it. This is also the case if someone holds up a big "I love you" sign and you happen to be blind; you won't receive that message because you don't have the capacity for receiving the message in the mode in which it was given, according to the media by which it was transmitted. If you can't read the story of the woman that Jesus has mercy on, or can't hear it, you will not be able to receive it.

7. The Act of Reception

The act of reception is the way in which you get the revelation. It is the exercising of the capacity. You hear the song; you see the blank screen. You may exercise your capacity or not. You may shut your eyes, stop up your ears, or simply not open the letter. The act of reception is your active part in revelation. It may be a passive act as you overhear something you didn't know, you read something without meaning to, or you bump into something in the dark. You may be willing or unwilling, but you are receiving the information.

A few simple points should be evident from this complex set of factors. The first is that if there is to be revelation from one person to another, five elements must be present. There must be a message, idea, or other form of revelation to be communicated, the way in which it is communicated, an available medium for that communication, a capacity to receive information through that medium on the part of the recipient, and the act of receiving. If any of these elements are not present, communication or revelation cannot happen. There can be no communication of Beethoven's Piano Sonata No. 8 to a rock that has neither the capacity nor the ability to exercise the capacity of hearing. I cannot communicate to you the beauty of this sonata, especially its second movement, through this text. You must hear it. This mode of communication isn't appropriate, and the media—black text on white paper or computer screen—cannot contain its loveliness.

Let us take as another example, something that can be contained here: the last five lines of Tennyson's *Ulysses*.

We are not now that strength which in old days
Moved earth and heaven, that which we are, we are;
One equal temper of heroic hearts,
Made weak by time and fate, but strong in will
To strive, to seek, to find, and not to yield.

You, as the reader, perhaps have all the capacities to receive the tragic and heroic beauty of this poem, but if you were to hand this book to an ape, or perhaps even read the poem aloud to it, the animal could not receive what is contained therein.

Apes may have a capacity for aesthetic beauty, but they don't have all the linguistic, poetic, mythic, historical, or philosophical capacities necessary to understand the art. If you were to hand the poem to a scholar of myth and lover of poetry who doesn't read English, they also would not be able to receive the glory of Tennyson's words. We return to the principle of *Quidquid recipitur*: whatever is received by someone is received according to their capacity to do so.

This principle, and the lack of our understanding of it in daily life, is behind many of the problems in our relationships. The principle functions between those who have just recently graduated with their PhDs and first-year undergraduates. The newly minted doctors of history, English, theology, and philosophy, wishing to demonstrate their vast knowledge, use terms and assumptions that their students don't have access to and so the information is not conveyed. The principle functions in relationships in which one partner gives over and over, but in a way that the other partner is incapable of receiving. It exists in social, often church, situations in which one person attempts to show their Christian love for another in a manner that may be uncomfortable or offensive to the receiver. In many of these situations, the giver can feel slighted or angry when their gift is not received in the way they intended. But, in all these cases, the principle of the *Quidquid recipitur* casts light on these muddled and confused communications.

By now, you might be asking what all of this has to do with sacraments, let alone video games. To answer that, I want to consider a few of the sacraments according to these seven elements. You may disagree with some of the ways that I break these things out, and that's fine, but I hope my point will be clear. It is worth saying that in all these sacraments, the revealer is God. And, primarily, that which is revealed is God. However, I will try to point to a particular aspect of God that is being revealed. Further, when it comes to the medium of revelation, the answer is also always "God." The Holy Spirit is the medium and the message. So, with every medium listed below, it is given as the material medium, or what philosophy might call the "instrumental cause" of the communication by the Holy Spirit. Further, while we have talked somewhat about information, generally it is not information that is revealed in the sacraments. Instead, God is revealed in a way that enacts God in our world. Sins are forgiven, and relationships healed; new relationships and capabilities are bestowed. The revelation of sacraments is, by revealing God and not merely information about God, a transformative revelation.

Baptism

2. The Thing Revealed/Enacted: that the person being baptized is now a member of the Body of Christ, that the wicked powers of the world and sin no longer have uncontested power over this person, and that they will rise with Christ on the last day.

3. The Mode of Revelation/Enactment: the pouring of water over the person, or immersion in water, and the speaking of the words, "I baptize you in the name of the Father, and the Son, and the Holy Spirit" by a person who has been baptized.

4. The Media of Revelation/Enactment: water and sound.

5. The Receiver: the person being baptized.

6. The Capacity for Reception: being alive, having not been baptized before.

7. The Act of Reception: having the water poured over the person, having the words said to them.

It is worth noting a few things about baptism. First, neither belief nor willingness are necessary for baptism. Forced baptisms are valid, though grievous sins. Second, having been baptized before prevents a person from receiving baptism again. As a teenager who thought it was wise to undergo "rebaptism" as I rebelled against my Catholic upbringing, I am aware of the problems involved in this choice. Further, the person need not have the capacity to hear, nor to understand, the words during the baptism. Baptism in Latin for a person who does not speak Latin is as valid as baptism in their native language. One needs to have the words said to them; they need not hear them.

Reconciliation

2. The Thing Revealed/Enacted: the person being reconciled is forgiven of their sins and once more in a right relationship with God.

3. The Mode of Revelation/Enactment: the repentance from and confession of sins, the pronouncement of absolution, and the sign of the cross.

4. The Media of Revelation/Enactment: sound and light.

5. The Receiver: the person confessing and being reconciled.

6. The Capacity for Reception: repentance, having been baptized into Christ.

7. The Act of Reception: being told that you have been forgiven, having the sign of the cross enacted for this sacrament.

Matrimony

2. The Thing Revealed/Enacted: that the two persons being joined are now, in a mysterious way, one flesh in Christ.

3. The Mode of Revelation/Enactment: the giving of vows to each other.

4. The Media of Revelation/Enactment: language, whether spoken, signed, or written.

5. The Receiver: the two persons who profess their vows to each other.

6. The Capacity for Reception: being free, sound-minded persons who intend their vows and are not bound by conflicting previous vows.

7. The Act of Reception: having vows reciprocated freely.

In Western Christianity it is not the minister who administers the sacrament of matrimony to the two persons being married. Instead, they administer the sacrament to each other. Thus, it is a more complex activity than baptism, and is more akin to reconciliation, which makes sense. Both sacraments are involved in highly complex relationships. Baptism rests on the fundamental imbalance of things between God and humanity. Reconciliation and Matrimony both function on the premise that there is a kind of equality. Spouses share total equality regarding their volition and importance in their joining together. Between God and humanity, there is a graced equality given by God that allows humans to come to God as their Parent.

The Eucharist

2. The Thing Revealed/Enacted: the eternal life of God for humanity.

3. The Mode of Revelation/Enactment: the blessing of bread and wine. The giving of this bread and wine as the food of eternal life.

4. The Media of Revelation/Enactment: Bread and Wine/ The Flesh and Blood of Christ.

5. The Receiver: the person eating the bread and/or drinking the wine.

6. The Capacity for Reception: being able to consume either or both bread and wine. Having been baptized.

7. The Act of Reception: eating and/or drinking the consecrated bread and/or wine.

You will notice here that I do not say "having been baptized and confessed." One can receive the Eucharist once one has been baptized and need not be, for all practical purposes, excommunicated until the first experience of reconciliation. It is here that my tradition in the Anglican Communion is more aligned with the Greek Orthodox church than the Catholic tradition. Further, I have tried to allow for the spectrum of beliefs about the Eucharist, from Transubstantiation to Calvin's understanding that the church is elevated by the Spirit into the presence of Christ. Both ends of this spectrum are encompassed in the Anglican expression of Christianity. One need not hold to a Thomistic/Aristotelian view to maintain that one feeds on the flesh and blood of Christ. Luther's view, which is perhaps closest to my own, maintains the true flesh and blood while ejecting the Aristotelian philosophy, is an agreeable position.

The three formal sacraments that I have not examined here fall under the same rules. Confirmation is a conclusion of Baptism, and in many churches is practiced within that rite. Its media are words and chrism. Ordinations are conveyed by physical contact and words. The ministrations to the sick and dying are enacted with chrism and words. Having examined these, I wish to turn to the question of which, if any, of these could be conveyed by virtual worlds to human beings.

The Virtual World and Sacraments

Considering what we have said about virtual worlds so far in this book, we remember our three-level image of reality. Our picture of these sacraments has been one that involves only the top two levels. God is the primary actor and God is the primary content that is communicated. The natural world, in one form or another, is the mode and media of this communication, and our natural and supernatural capacities allow us to receive these communications or revelations. If we are to receive sacraments through virtual worlds, we must ask whether they are adequate tertiary media to transmit the secondary media of the sacrament in a way appropriate to our capacities to receive the sacrament. This must be our criterion for each sacrament in a virtual world. If the virtual can provide an adequate medium for the existing media of a sacrament, then it seems possible that that sacrament could be administered through the virtual. If the virtual cannot provide an adequate medium, then the sacrament is not possible through the virtual.

Immediately we find that any sacrament that relies primarily or solely on sound or language for its media seems possible. Take, for example, reconciliation. In a situation in which I am seated in my pew and confessing my sins, or in a more traditional "one-on-one" confessional, the media that convey my words, the priest's words, and the priest's actions to me are air and light. Again, primarily the medium here is the Holy Spirit as the One who both carries the message and is the message. On the secondary natural level, I speak words, the priest speaks words, signs the cross, and I am reconciled to God.

If this is the case, we must ask whether it is appropriate that I can do these things at some distance from the priest, and whether physical barriers create a problem. If I am in the front row of the church, clearly, I am within the range of the act of confession. But what if I am in the far back corner of the large church? Surely the activity of the Spirit is not hindered by my seating placement. No one, as far as I can tell, would argue that this is the case, nor would they argue that my confession and absolution are somehow incrementally less effective than those of the lady in the front pew. What about the folks in the daycare downstairs? If they receive an audio or video stream and they confess with the rest of the congregation, will they not receive the same absolution? It would seem hard to say that they will not. If they cannot, who would trade the absolution of God for the care of children? Is that even a real choice? Do we believe that the Spirit says, "The bounds of these walls are the limits of intention and sacramental reality, no one who is beyond these four stone/wood/plaster walls can be included in this confession and absolution?" If one would argue this, I would find it hard to understand, given that the media of the sacrament, the capacity, and the act of reception are all entirely possible within the bounds of a streamed service to the room below.

Given this, we ask about whether such a confession is possible then over the web. Could I sit at my computer with my priest, see her over Skype, tell her my sins, hear her absolution, receive the sign of the cross, and be reconciled to God? Again, all the elements of the sacrament are present. I confess, I have the words of reconciliation spoken to me, and the media that convey them convey them adequately. What then should prevent me from receiving sacramental grace?

The objection might arise that we are distant from each other, but what does this matter? If the media of technology allow us to transmit, without significant interference or loss, the mode and media of the sacrament as required, then there should be no impediment. This goes as well for the presentation of a person in a virtual environment. I might meet my priest in a virtual confessional, speak words that she hears, hear her pronouncement of God's forgiveness, and see her avatar make the sign of the cross as it mimics her own hand movements. The sensual and somatic information is conveyed to me in practically the same way that it would be in person, though the things conveying that information allow us to do so from a distance. Some might object at this point that we do not see the person's body but only a digital representation and therefore the words and somatic rituals are not really being done to us. But this is not a real impediment to the sacrament, as much of the sacrament's history has existed in situations where the person making their confession and the confessor might not see each other.

One might also say, "I just don't like the whole thing. It's too impersonal." Fears of people sitting in their rooms, cut off from real-world experiences, only interfacing with a world through their virtual reality goggles can rear their heads here. Visions of E. M. Forster's "The Machine Stops" flood into our minds as we picture lumps of pale flesh seated in their comfortable chairs surrounded by buttons that can call for everything:

> Then she generated the light, and the sight of her room, flooded with radiance and studded with electric buttons, revived her. There were buttons and switches everywhere— buttons to call for food for music, for clothing. There was the hot-bath button, by pressure of which a basin of (imitation) marble rose out of the floor, filled to the brim with a warm deodorized liquid. There was the cold-bath button. There was the button that produced literature. And there were of course the buttons by which she communicated with her friends. The room, though it contained nothing, was in touch with all that she cared for in the world.[3]

Even though it was first published in 1909, this picture by Forster still encompasses our fears of technological isolation. Our fear of encouraging and promoting the kind of existence that Forster predicted is worthwhile and should be ever at our side when we consider the choices we want to make for our society. We may insist that, while such a confession would be possible, it might not be advisable for the common person. But there are plenty of extenuating circumstances in which such a

---

3. E. M. Forester, "The Machine Stops," *The Oxford and Cambridge Review*, November 1909.

confession is the best expedient. Take, for example, the congregant who has gone to her church her whole life, who loves the shape and structure of the building, and who remembers walking its aisles, but now can only walk in her memories. She is restricted to a chair. The ideal situation, of course, would be to be able to bring her to the church, but what if this isn't possible? What if weekly confessional visits are also impractical? Knowing that the sacrament can be validly conveyed by means of the virtual could be helpful in this situation.

Therefore, I think that sacraments that are communicated by actions directed at another person but do not require physical contact, such as Reconciliation and Matrimony, can be administered by way of the virtual. However, the rest require not only somatic ritual, but physical media to convey the mode of revelation.

Let us take Baptism, for example. In the real world a person has water applied to them in some fashion and the trinitarian formula of baptism spoken over them. Their own body meets the water that is the media of the Holy Spirit's specific revelation of God, namely the incorporation of that person's flesh into the life of the Resurrected Christ. This is not primarily a sacrament that makes a person feel something, nor a sacrament that mainly affects their internal identity. This is an action that sanctifies their flesh that has now passed through water that has incorporated them into the death of Christ and given them a share in His resurrection.

In a virtual setting, something very different is happening. If I enter a virtual world and my representation there (my avatar) has virtual water poured over their head by the avatar of another person, the whole structure of the sacrament falls to pieces. The mode of revelation is not present. No water is poured over my head. Perhaps the person on the other side of the other avatar has been baptized, and perhaps they have said the trinitarian formula to me, but for it to be a valid baptism, they must pour water over me. The media, water and sound, are only half present. Finally, I am not able perform the act of reception. I cannot have the water poured over me.

Further, no water is poured over the head of the avatar, nor does the avatar receive baptism according to its nature. That is not real water, even by analogy. It is only water by a fictional simulacrum. There is no "pouring" or "applying" happening. Instead, a complex animation is taking place, like the animation of water falling on Daffy Duck in a cartoon. Three-dimensional virtual water is no more water than two-dimensional artistic images of water. Both are artistic representations that have only the most surface level similarities to the actual substance.

We might ask, given the situation of the person mentioned above, can we not make a provision for this person regarding baptism? What if she longs to be baptized but simply cannot? Are the waters of regeneration to be denied to her? No, but we must not confuse ourselves about this. First, there is already a provision for her in the concept of the "baptism of desire." A person wishing to be baptized, but who has not had the opportunity, is accepted in the grace of Christ as if they were baptized. If the opportunity arises in which she can be baptized, she must take it, otherwise the question of the validity of her "desire" arises. Second, no one will do her any good by providing her with a ritual that does not actually effect the desired outcome. The Holy Spirit works through baptism in a precise way for a precise effect. Sacraments are not generic encounters with the Holy Spirit. They are unique encounters with God that take unique historical shapes. If one were to provide this unfortunate woman with a "virtual baptism," then one not only deceives her about what baptism is, but also prevents her from receiving actual baptism later since she believes she already has it. "Will God not provide for her, after having been deceived?" we might ask. We trust that God would, but it certainly shouldn't be the business of the church to be willfully enacting deceptions trusting that God will "sort it all out in the end."

In the Eucharist, we have a more complex reality to consider. The content of the communication in this sacrament is the eternal life of God to humanity. The mode of this revelation and enactment is the bread and wine, which become the flesh and blood of Christ. It is especially important when it comes to Baptism and the Eucharist to remember that the unique character of these sacraments comes from the lived life of Jesus of Nazareth. They are historically rooted in his actions and have their mode and media because they were chosen by him to communicate the grace that they do. There are no substitutes for the mode and media of this sacrament.

The act of reception is eating and drinking of consecrated bread and wine. This means that for a person to receive the Eucharist, they must indeed eat this bread and/or drink this wine. They are gifts given to humanity in the mode of food and drink in this reality. When we consider how a virtual Eucharist might work, we are presented with two general possibilities: remote Eucharist by means of video-chat, or virtual Eucharist participated in in a video game–like setting. I want to consider each separately.

Remote Eucharist

Let's imagine a situation where a person can't come to church for whatever reason. They wish to participate in the Eucharist with their congregation but are unable to do so. They turn on their computer, watch the service, confess with their congregation, and set out bread and wine in front of their laptop. When the pastor consecrates the elements, they understand that consecration to include their bread and wine. When the time comes to commune, they eat and drink. Such Eucharists have taken place already in our world. But are they valid?

Certainly, all the elements of the sacrament are there. Words, bread, wine, eating, and drinking. The priest consecrates the elements, and the person receives them. If our earlier argument about confession is correct, then the distance between the person and their congregation does not matter. The real question is the relationship between the bread and wine on the little plate in front of the monitor and the bread and wine on the altar. Do these elements fall under the sacramental transformation that encompasses the bread and wine on the altar?

Before we tackle that question as it relates to someone sitting in a house, miles away, we might ask about a much less complex situation. Imagine that the priest has consecrated bread and wine at the altar, but, during the administration of the sacrament, they run out. The sacristy isn't far and it has more. When it is retrieved, must it be sanctified on the altar, or shall we assume that God has provided for the people in any case? How we answer this question affects how we answer this version of the remote Eucharist question. I know a Lutheran minister and scholar who would argue that no new consecration was necessary. I know others who would say that it is. In the Catholic tradition, a whole new Mass must be said from the beginning. Let us see if we can figure out which is correct.

My understanding of the position that says that you don't have to consecrate new bread and wine is that it maintains that God will provide for the people despite the priest's lack of preparation. That the Lord will provide is an essential element of Christian faith. It also forms the essential confidence that we have in the sacraments, particularly in the Catholic expression of the idea of *ex opere operato* ("from the work performed"). We have confidence in our sacraments not because we rely on the faith of the priest or even on our own faith at that moment but because God has promised to be present when the sacrament is performed properly. A person does not need to believe in Jesus to be baptized, nor does the person who is baptizing them. If the one performing the baptism has been baptized, and performs the baptism correctly, it is a valid baptism. Thus, an unbelieving or heretic priest can present every sacrament validly. We need not worry whether we are receiving forgiveness, healing, or the Eucharist depending on whether or not our priest is going through a crisis of faith.

Does this transfer to the bread in the other room if the priest doesn't intend to consecrate it? We could get technical on the question of intention. Perhaps the priest has placed the bread on the altar and is going through a very bad point in their life. They don't want the bread to consecrate and intend that it won't. They still say the words, so we know that despite their ill intentions, the bread still is the flesh of Christ for the people.

It is, perhaps, safer to say that the bread and wine that the church presents before God is the bread and wine that the church intends to be consecrated. In this case, only the bread and wine on the altar is encompassed in that intention. They are the gifts presented to God. The bread in the other room isn't intended to be given to God. In this case, if there isn't enough, more would have to be consecrated.

What of the gift placed before God remotely by the person who is sitting at their computer? Does this count as included on the altar? I think, under a very special circumstance, it does. And that special circumstance is that the congregation specifically intends to include the small loaf of bread and the sip of wine that's sitting on the woman's desk. These offerings of bread and wine then are the offerings of the congregation and are covered under the priest's sacramental words and actions. This, however, doesn't cover a situation where the person simply turns on a webcam stream anonymously, places bread and wine in front of their monitor, waits for the words of consecration, and then eats and drinks. These gifts are not included;

they were not offered by the congregation, but by an individual. It seems then that they are not included in the sacramental act of the church.

Avatars Communing

Just as virtual water is not water, virtual bread and wine are not bread and wine. Nor is it the case that when an avatar puts a piece of virtual bread in their virtual mouth and open and close their virtual jaws, the act of eating is involved. Everything is a simulacrum—a fake dressed up to look like the real thing. The problem becomes easier when we ask whether a painting of people receiving Eucharist contains painted people who are receiving painted grace by means of painted bread. The problem, however, seems much bigger because avatars move in ways that remind us of our own world, but the reality is that the similarities are happening in our own minds. The actual existences of digital persons are nothing like real humans. We might make the art so that it resembles humans. As of the writing of this book, Magic Leap's Mica is perhaps the closest thing to a virtual person that has tricked my mind. I could be fooled by Mica because her creators made her to trick my mind. But it is a trick.

That is not to say that a programmer couldn't design a virtual world where virtual actors in the world go to church, enact reconciliation, perform actions that look like eating and drinking, and receive programmed benefits from these actions. One can easily imagine a *Sims* expansion called *Sims Worship* where the sims could go to a mosque, a Buddhist temple, or a synagogue and receive numerical benefits from these experiences. Their social numbers might go up, their stress might go down; indeed, an overall wellness bonus might be given. But the programmers would be the ones deciding how that all works. God would not grant grace to imaginary people because they are programmed to enact imaginary versions of human life.

When our characters do these things, we might say that "we" did them, but we must remember our reflections on the Chalcedonian formula. We do them according to the nature in which they happened. When the game *BioShock Infinite* came out, there were people who got upset because they felt they had been baptized at the beginning of the game when the main character is immersed and baptized in the name of the founders of the fantastical city, Columbia. Even ignoring the fact that the baptism in the game doesn't meet the requirements of Christianity, the player has not been subjected to anything like baptism. The character has fictionally undergone this treatment, and we might say that "we" have undergone it, but we have undergone it according to the nature of the virtual. Since we are not bound to these virtual representations in the way that the Second Person of the Trinity has irrevocably bound himself to humanity, the actions do not rise to the level of creating our identity. If they did, then the act of killing dozens of people in Columbia, or in any game, would present a problem at least as significant as an inadequately performed baptism. Thus, we run into the limitations of our identification with the virtual, as well as return to the question of the ethics of actions in the virtual. Unless they arise to the level of the real, they remain ethically vacant.

Conclusion

We must not be fooled by our ever-increasing ability to create virtual representations that appear to be real. We are on the verge of making virtual worlds so real that we cannot tell the difference by sight and sound; we must not be swept up by the talents of artists and the technical expertise of programmers. Many gamers have already developed empathy and other strong feelings for fictional characters. This is good and right only as far as it goes. Most of us have loved fictional characters that are well written, whether Poirot for his cleverness, affability, and fastidiousness, Watson for his loyalty and heartiness, or Princess Leia for her bravery, intelligence, and leadership. We love fictional characters, but we must not lose sight of the fact that they exist in that world below and we cannot bring them up. They are real, but they are real according to their natures. Like George C. Scott's Scrooge, we might chuckle and shake our heads at anyone who says they are not real, but we must admit what kind of reality they have and not lose sight of the hierarchy of reality for the sake of our own reality.

SCOUTING THINGS OUT
FOR FUTURE
EXPLORATIONS

I've been exploring the austere landscape of the island region of Morrowind for weeks. The world has captured me in the way that only your first truly open-world fantasy role-play game can. I am enchanted by the seemingly living reality that suggests thousands of years of history, the loss of an entire race of people to a magical cataclysm, and the threat of a powerful and ancient enemy overwhelming the world.

I've been wandering the western lands and have met a small settlement of elves. They indicate to me, as best as I can remember, that there are ancestral burial caves to the east somewhere. I seek them out and find myself in a labyrinthine complex of underground passages. There are shelves and nooks high up that I can only get to if I use magic, and the mummified corpses of heroes belonging to a bygone age. Each is arrayed in different armor and weapons. Most are mundane, but some are magical.

The tombs are expansive, and my exploration is permeated with a sense of wonderful dread. The undead roam the caves, but so does my imagination. What could I find next? Who is this hero who is set here in honor with her weapons set at her side? Where do I fit into this heritage of bravery and glory?

Possible Ways Forward

The *Elder Scrolls III: Morrowind* presented me with many memorable experiences in cities and ruins that remain real to me. Some stand out, like meeting the last living dwarf in what equates to a leper colony, but one stands above the rest. It is an experience that, for me, all other moments of exploration in video games are invariably measured against.

I have journeyed in many worlds. I have seen wonders created by many people, but in all my wanderings, no place has enthralled me so much as those caves where mighty heroes were laid to rest. Perhaps one day I will return there again.

This chapter is intended as a brief introduction to areas where theology might go in its consideration of video games. It is exploratory, and likely in need of significant criticism. It should be taken as a jumping-off point for discussion, not a hard-and-fast prescription for how the church should go forward. There are some ideas here, like the redemption of play, that exist already in parts of the gaming world and in significant parts of play in other areas. Others engage ideas that are only beginning to appear in our approach to games, the world, and the virtual. All are submitted as possible paths of consideration.

The Redemption of Play

There are many definitions of play, but my own is that play is finding delight in limitations. All forms of play are predicated on the fact that we are not limitless beings who can do whatever we want. This joy from limitation may be expressed as simply pretending that a hill is Mt. Everest and that we are great explorers to games of jacks, chess, baseball, or *Frogger*. We delight in working within sets of limitations, attempting to be excellent in the face of challenges, and succeeding in adversity.

Competitive play adds the far more exciting limitation of the struggle of other people against us. How much better to sword-fight your brother with large foam swords than to swing your sword at imaginary goblins. How much greater the fun when he passes my guard with a surprise attack and gets me right in the gut. No imaginary pirate could actually outwit me, though I might pretend she did.

The goal of play is joy. We engage in play to harvest joy. If we are playing against others and we are generous, we hope that the other persons gather joy for themselves out of the experience. When play is co-opted by some other impulse, the goal of play is undermined. One of the three greatest co-opters of play is the goal of victory. We have so ingrained in our culture that victory is the end of play that we might revolt at the idea that play is essentially not about winning. We might think that the idea is quaint and cute, and if you want to play to have fun then go play with the "losers."

The other co-opters of play are fame and profit. Play is not seen as a means to joy, but instead as a means to money or fame. Of these three—fame, money, and play—only play is holy and eternal. For it is play that will have its home in the coming age. Our natural play will be crowned with perfected and supernatural play in the age to come, while our wealth and fame will fade away. To redeem play, the church must ask what part it will have in the play of the world. Will its organized play, which is largely associated with sport, and rarely with, say, a chess league, focus on the joy given in playing, or will it take worldly pride in having the "best" teams and encourage the kinds of behaviors that parents teach their children when they seek to rob children of the delight of play in order to make them exceptional athletes? Will the church take the side of the natural end of play, or will it help to co-opt it?

Lest someone who reads this think that I am suggesting we should simply play freeform games without score, I must add that I believe that redeemed competition—the kind of competition that seeks to do its very best and that encourages its opponents to do their very best—is aided by keeping score and seeing who wins. There are those who would rather just throw a ball or a Frisbee around or play the freeform scoreless games of Free-for-All in *Halo* or *Call of Duty*. These things have their place. But scoring, victory, and loss add elements to the game that allow players to draw out new and exciting kinds of excellence and joy. There can be no rally, no comeback, no genius stratagem if no one is keeping score. No one could ever feel the galvanizing force of their teammates working together against great odds to eke out a victory, either total or moral, after being dominated. No one could feel the wonder at seeing their opponents rally, or feel the momentum of their excellence build and, in the end, triumph. Without score and without challenge, we would not be called to the greater excellence that can unlock greater wells of capability and therefore, greater expanses of joy. These are joys available to us only when we play within limits and when we add the concepts of score and competition. But we must master these ideas, not let them master us. Victory and defeat must serve joy, not some other end; otherwise we have undone the concept of play.

There are, of course, plenty of situations in which we play where there can be no score, no winner, and no loser. No one won when my brother and I, as boys, fought "the invisible men" in our backyard, pool, or bedroom. No one wins in a game of *Dungeons & Dragons*. Indeed, no one wins in a game of hacky sack, which I loved in high school. In all these, the joy of play is present without competition. We must neither bow to the masters of victory and loss nor abandon them for competition-free games exclusively. The church must claim all things for Christ, including competition.

Chivalric Reclamation

One of the most brutal facts of gaming is that the community of gamers can often be factional and abusive. There is a tendency to draw lines, to take allegiance with famous personalities, games, or, perhaps most monstrously, with corporations and their products. This tendency toward factionalism, while not unfamiliar in the history and practice of Christianity, is contrary to the heart of Christ. Certainly, the vilification and demeaning of those who love something different than what we love is madness. The process of "othering," so prominent throughout human history, reaches one of its great pinnacles of pettiness when one group of people who like to play games on one product mock and vilify those who like to do the same thing, only on a different product. Such a state of affairs is in desperate need of reordering. One area into which we might apply ourselves is the reviving of the Christian conception of chivalry. I do not mean what is popularly known as chivalry, which involves acts like men opening doors for women, but instead an ordered dedication of service to God, persons, and, especially, the weak.

The calls of modern social justice are largely consonant with the ideals of chivalry, especially when one considers the knight's dedication to those who could not defend themselves. However, the role of true chivalry bolsters some of the weaker points of the social justice movement, especially around charitable care for enemies. The service of chivalric ideals requires certain modifications, however, considering our contemporary situation. While the old ideals of chivalry sought for male knights to serve a single lady first, and then all women after, a contemporary revitalization of chivalric ideals should be one of defense for empowerment. Taken from the perspective that men, especially in the world of gaming, continue to have the most power in all areas (business, creative, and consumption), though they do not represent the majority in all those areas. A chivalric reclamation would be an attempt by those dedicated to serving God to defend those who undergo aggressions to empower them. For this to be a truly Christian movement in gaming culture, it must avoid the deadly trap of othering those who do the attacking. The true Christian chivalric ideal is one that may have to challenge, confront, and struggle against the efforts of another person or group of people, but never to treat them with less than dignity, honor, and the love of Christ. Given such a proposal, three considerations immediately arise.

First, one imagines a group of male gamers taking to social media, slapping on the label of "Gaming Knight," and rushing to the aid of anyone who is verbally attacked on Twitter, Facebook, or other social media. These well-meaning and perhaps somewhat self-aggrandized lads would, almost certainly, become insufferable immediately. The heart of chivalry is not doffing one's cap and addressing someone as "m'lady," but is instead humble and brave service to one's neighbor. An online self-styled policing brigade is not what I here proposing.

Second, the heart of this movement is largely in-person and must be enacted with actual bravery. It must involve a confrontation of toxicity in all aspects of society, though we are focusing on the gaming community. It involves the bravery of men in the workplace to stand up for female colleagues to create a gaming community in which men standing up for women is no longer necessary. This pattern is true for race, age, and gender. It means possibly putting one's job, reputation, and perhaps career on the line. It involves bravery.

Third, the concept of the ideals of knighthood, even in this debunking age, may be wildly appealing to gamers who regularly direct knights or their equivalents on virtual battle-fields. While we may exist in a post–*Game of Thrones* age in which knighthood is largely mocked and undermined, we are not incapable of reclaiming the ideals of those who, having been prepared and dedicated to God, went out into the world looking to serve. Of course, this spirit already exists in the community. My suggestion is that it should be galvanized as a Christian force for humble and brave service in opposition to forces that dehumanizes through anonymity, racism, and gender discrimination.

The Gamification of Orders

In her book *Reality Is Broken*, Jane McGonigal suggests that the "gamification" of jobs and life makes things better. She explains the difficulties inherent in the tension between a job that you work at for three years and never see any progress despite your best efforts and a video game in which you frequently level up and are consistently rewarded for your hard work. Her suggestion to gamifying life is one that rests, to some degree, on the same psychological foundations as the design of casino games. Positive feedback is powerful and keeps us going at whatever it is that we are doing.

Long before Professor McGonigal proposed her ideas, there were organizations that understood the concepts of leveling up and awarding achievements. Groups like the Masons, the military, and the Boy Scouts have all understood that ascending in ranks, receiving badges and medals, and having new titles all are impressive motivators. It's also worth noting that for these organizations, the ranks and badges are intrinsically not the point; they support the main point. The goal of the Scouts has never been to accumulate as many badges as possible and to achieve the highest rank possible. Nor has the point of the U.S. Army, for example, been to rise to the highest rank and to accumulate the greatest number of medals. Each organization has its own integral goal. Each understands that there are psychological and social motivators that can elevate the excellence of those involved. I suggest that a similar process might be enacted within religious and lay orders in the church. There are, of course, some groups that already do this, like the Knights of Columbus. However, the creation of new charitable orders, perhaps with catchy and inspiring names, that honor the achievements of their members in a public way, might find great success. In the digital age, integrating these into existing achievement systems would be highly beneficial.

Of course, the response might be, "If we are doing charity to earn badges or achievements or to level up, then we are doing things for the wrong reasons." That's true. If we join an organization and do good so we can garner as many awards as possible, we are doing it for the wrong reasons. Again, let me point to the organizations that have done this for centuries. Perhaps there are some people who join the military to earn as many medals, patches, and badges as they can, but there are far more who join to serve their country, and find among the traditions of the military, including the giving of badges to signal achievements, an expression of excellence, honor, and inspiration.

My grandfather, for example, was a paratrooper in the 82nd Airborne Division during World War II. I don't believe he decided to jump out of a perfectly good airplane, and undergo the toughest military training available at the time, just to get a pin with wings and a parachute on it. I wouldn't be surprised, based on the accounts I have read of other paratroopers, that at some point in the grueling training, that pin, or the ability to blouse his pants over his boots like a paratrooper—both signs of great accomplishment—inspired him. He didn't join for those reasons, but that simple sign of achievement inspired men like him to tough it out, do the hard thing, and keep going.

Taking these methods into practice for the church need not be flashy and need not disobey Christ's command to "not let our left hand know what our right hand is doing." We need not level up to demonstrate our charity. There are ways other than a gold badge for donating money or time to mark achievement, dedication, and excellence. We can acknowledge innovation, excellence in the development of skills, and leadership. We can also acknowledge humility and the building up of others. Modeling the image of kings who are given crowns by God but who then cast them back at God's feet should be the goal in such honors.

There might also be some objection to the use of military-style achievement in religious settings. There are objections leveled against video games, beyond the violence that is so often mentioned, that they are based on computational architecture that was developed by the military for military means. In this view, the very manner of processing information is somehow bent toward a militaristic mindset.

I find these arguments largely unconvincing for two reasons: first, the application of the principle in other areas of life does not seem to be true and, second, that the digitizing of already existing activities does not make them more militaristic. In the first case, let us take the development of the airplane. Certainly, the Wright brothers didn't develop the airplane for the military, but aircraft, as well as rocketry and space exploration, were developed largely for military application. I see no particularly military character to a local pilot going up in a Cessna to fly for pleasure or a commercial flight leaving a major airport. There certainly are technologies in use that were developed with and by the military, but their application does not bend toward the military simply for that reason.

Regarding the second reason, many activities that already existed, such as writing, playing games, and doing accounting, have been ported over to computers without any "militarizing" effect. I may be writing more efficiently with my word processing application than a Sumerian with his clay tablet and reed, but the process is essentially the same. There is nothing more violent or militaristic in my writing than in his. The games of chess, checkers, and solitaire have all come over to computers whole cloth without somehow becoming more violently ordered. The same can be said of arrays of different business practices like accounting and record keeping

I also find it unconvincing that employing lessons learned from one sector of life to another will somehow necessarily make the recipient more like the donor except in ways related to the thing carried over. Bringing over achievements and badges and similar items from the military will no more make religious organizations militaristic than it will make them efficient in making campfires. We may employ the metaphors of those other sectors, but then so did St. Paul without turning toward violence. Hiding ourselves from certain ideas because they can go wrong is akin to building a hedge around the Torah. The better path here is to know where the pitfalls are, to learn from the past, and to go forward with fortitude and prudence. Again, this is not an original idea, by any means, but it seems that, especially in an age of ubiquitous technology, phone apps, and social media, compassion in conjunction with the giving of achievements, badges, and such honors seems as if it could be highly beneficial.

A Joyful Church

What if the church was the place where people played? What if it was the place where the people who are geeks, meaning the people who love things in the world not because they are idols but because they speak to them at their very core, were so welcomed that there was a sense of real community? What if the church delivered on its promise of being a truly human institution along with being truly divine?

One might argue that the church currently is truly human and that's not going so well. What we need is for the church to be more divine. Yes, the church could use more divinization and partaking in God's nature. But I don't agree that the church is too human. I'd say that it isn't human enough. Jesus was truly human and showed us what true humanity looks like. In 1965, the Roman Catholic church succinctly put this in the *Pastoral Constitution on the Church in the Modern World*, *Gaudium et Spes*, saying, "Christ, the final Adam, by the revelation of the mystery of the Father and His love, fully reveals man to man himself and makes his supreme calling clear." Our faults are subhuman; they lower us below the stature of Christ. We need true humanity in our churches, and that true humanity includes play.

I don't think that there is any one kind of play that is genuinely superior to another. Football is not better than video games, nor are video games better than Mahjong. All have their corruptions; all have their innocent joys. Church must be a place where play is welcomed and enjoyed if it is to be place where the summation of our natural loves and joys meets the summation of our supernatural loves and joys. We must be able to lay our games on the altar of God and say, "Make our play holy," for the fact is, we will play. We must play, lest we take ourselves and our lives too seriously. I don't mean the church should be frivolous. We must pray together, build each other up, and mourn together. We should also be joyful people, not merely participating in that joy of the Spirit which is the gift of God, but joyful in our play together, whether with video games, tabletop games, ultimate Frisbee, or Canasta.

Few worship experiences have been better in my life than those that I share with people who share common interests. We worship well together because we have learned to care for each other through what we share in common. Many of those have been experiences of play. We can be solemn together because we can also be silly together. And we can be silly because we can be solemn. We can be human together. That is also not to say that church should become cliquish or a place where we only meet people with common interests. One of the church's great virtues, by being human, is that it puts together people that the culture would keep apart: the young and the old, the rich and the poor, the insider and the disenfranchised. When it doesn't do this, it fails to be truly human. But the church must be a place where we can share our natural joys so that we can lift them up together. And, I submit, video games are one of those joys the church should be celebrating and working together to make holy.

New Game+: The Virtual Person

Finally, I am bringing together the two areas with which I have spent the most time in my academic career: virtual worlds and eschatology. I have written articles on the questions surrounding Christian eschatology, and the question about the integrity of human identity in the resurrection of the dead is an important one. "Will I be truly myself when I am raised from the dead?" is one that has occupied the minds of Christian thinkers since at least the second century.

Early questions centered around the difficulty of God reassembling all the same matter that once made up our bodies. In the medieval period, the problem moved to the supernatural realm, as human identity was largely stashed in the immortality of the soul. More recent questions have arisen regarding the problems of disability, physicality, and relational identity. Will we remain ourselves if we are raised fundamentally other than we were, either regarding conditions like Down syndrome, or in a world without the plant and animal life that we are deeply related to, or even without certain people who make us who we are?

Further questions arise around the human integration of technology. If I have lived with technological implants my whole life, will they be raised with me? If I have lived in augmented reality my whole life, will that be included in my resurrected experience of the world? If not, is it really the historical "me" that has been raised, or some reassembled abstracted idea of human nature with my consciousness? What if I spend my whole life in a virtual world? What relationship do I have to the physical world I never interacted with? What if I spend my time in several virtual worlds? Will they rise with me? Will they be given a greater existence because I have been given a greater existence?

If our answer is a default "no" to all these things, and that resurrection is a more serious and "real" event than these questions might imply, we must ask where we are drawing our line regarding the integrity of the person who is raised. Is it human nature, unmodified and "pure" that is raised, and we are merely instances of it? If so, in what way do I have any authorship over my identity? Put another way, are human beings essentially just instances of an abstract nature, or are they essentially historical particular beings who are not able to be separated from their existence as ones who enact human nature in distinct ways and in distinct relationships?

C. S. Lewis proposed the resurrection of certain pets in *The Problem of Pain*, if they were elevated to a near personhood by the good master in the good household. Is that possible for the fictional or the virtual? Do these human creations hitch a ride into the divine life through us? If they are inherently sinful, they do not, but if they are not, if they are natural, and therefore rooted in the eternal goodness of God, then it may be that Middle Earth, Narnia, Hogwarts, and even the world of *Zork* might find themselves manifest as part of the new heavens and new earth, for they took part in the old heavens and old earth and added a few unique chords to the great music of joy that is, as C. S. Lewis points out, the serious business of heaven.

CONCLUSION

There are no topics beyond the scope of theological inquiry. We cannot leave the study of and engagement with any area of human existence aside. If we define theology as many Catholic institutions have, by quoting Anselm, as "faith seeking understanding," then we must apply this pursuit of understanding from the stance of faith to all things. Personally, I prefer to define theology as obedience to Christ's command to love God with the entirety of our minds. That means loving God through thinking about God, but also loving God through thinking about everything else.

Video games may seem frivolous at best and dangerous at worst. We may think that they are appealing to our baser or less ethical natures. We might call them "murder trainers" or toys used to teach us how to commit other acts of moral and practical evil. But the reality is that most people who play games are the same kinds of people who read popular fiction, play other kinds of popular games, and who have played at being soldiers, astronauts, and explorers for generations.

Video games are, barring catastrophe, here to stay and we in the church must consider our stance toward them. Christians are playing video games. Christians are engaging in both ethical and unethical behavior as they play. We cannot simply treat video games as childish, verboten, or obscene any longer. My goal in this book has been to present an argument for why and how we should pay attention to video games, first by way of introduction to some of the ideas surrounding games themselves, and then by considering how they can help us to think more clearly about what we already believe.

In many ways, video games can function for us as the angelic world did for the scholastic theologians. It seems rather nonsensical to me to adhere to many of the affirmations about angelic nature that one finds in the work of people like Thomas Aquinas, who made rather strong statements about angelic nature. We find there that angels have free will, but that their free will is frozen after their initial choice for God or self. We find that they are pure intelligences. We find that they exist in a temporal state between eternity and our own temporal existence. Indeed, we find that each angel is its own species. All these affirmations were solutions to problems presented by revelation.

Such strong statements about the free wills, natures, and species of beings that we know so little about seem audacious, but they are useful as thought experiments. The angelic world functioned for the scholastic mind much like a theological laboratory. The angels were the great material upon which the scholastic mind practiced its experiments. We may mock their pursuit by evoking the question, "How many angels can dance on the head of a pin?" but such questions are useful, if not for learning about angelic nature, then for learning about logic and possible natures.

It is in such a way that video games can be useful to the theological mind now. We can model realities in virtual worlds, show how they can work, and test our theories against them. We can compare Christological models, models of creation, of knowledge, and of relations. We can ask questions about revelation and divinization. We can test these ideas against the virtual to see where they fail and where they succeed. But just as the angelic experimentations of the "dark ages" don't really tell us much about angels themselves, so, too, will our models of theological concepts be limited when applied to video games.

We can get a good idea about how a nature might work when nestled inside of another nature, and how two natures might relate to each other when they are both inside of a third, larger nature, but these models don't tell us anything about how our world was made, or what great power it is that God uses to cause our cosmos and the world of the angels to interact.

Finally, lest anyone suppose that I am suggesting that video games have not been studied by religious people up to this point, let me say that there is a growing study of video games specifically in the field of religious studies. There have not been many works of theology, however, that have focused on video games, and, overall, the view in the academic world is strikingly like that of the pulpit. The rich fields of the virtual remain largely untilled, and their fruits remain occult. There is a harvest to be had. The only question that remains is when the reapers will come, and whether we must wait until those who have closed their minds have gone the way of those who condemned musical instruments, jazz, rock and roll, and other forms of popular media.

CPSIA information can be obtained
at www.ICGtesting.com
Printed in the USA
LVHW050943190122
708698LV00016B/2141